27 Fiction Writing Blunders—And How Not To Make Them!

⚬⚬⚬

27 Fiction Writing Blunders—
And How Not To Make Them!

James Scott Bell

Compendium Press

Compendium Press
P.O. Box 705
Woodland Hills, CA 91365

ISBN 10: 0-910355-25-8
ISBN 13: 978-0-910355-25-4

Table of Contents

Avoiding the Flubs of Fiction

They see them all day long.

Agents and editors—whose job it is to find authors and manuscripts of promise—are used to spotting the most common errors of fiction writers. These mistakes, most of which are easily avoidable, spell probable doom for a project under consideration.

Readers see these errors, too. While most readers are not schooled in the craft of fiction, they nevertheless *feel* something is off. Their reading pleasure is dampened. If that happens too much, they are less likely to finish the book.

Or seek out another from the same writer.

When I teach workshops, I refer to these blunders as "speed bumps." If you're taking a nice drive through beautiful country, you luxuriate in the view. You don't think about the road. You don't think much at all. You *enjoy*.

But if you hit a speed bump, it jolts you out of your reverie. It then takes you several moments to get back into flow, into enjoying the view once more.

But what if another speed bump comes along?

Then another?

In fact, what if this whole stretch of road is filled with bumps and potholes and the occasional traffic-blocking cow?

You don't enjoy the drive at all! You get irritated. You go home and yell at the dog.

To help save the dogs, make it your aim to keep readers *entranced*. You want to put them into a dreamlike state, so when they are reading the story they are not even conscious of reading; they are only conscious of *experiencing*.

We've all read books that did that for us. And we also

know how rare it is. I remember the first time it happened to me. It was reading a Classics Illustrated comic book. These were a staple of my youth, wonderful renderings of classic books in comic book form.

The one that enraptured me was *The Hunchback of Notre Dame*. I still remember the emotional impact when I finished it.

Later, when I started reading actual novels, I was caught up in stories like *Tarzan of the Apes* and *Dune*.

You have your favorite titles, too.

And as a writer, you want readers to feel the same way.

Which means writing with voice and passion and craft and care—and learning to recognize and eliminate those dang speed bumps!

In my book, *How to Make a Living as a Writer*, I included a chapter on the five biggest fiction writing mistakes. It was hard to keep it to five, but for the sake of brevity I did so.

But I kept thinking of more blunders writers need to identify, more speed bumps to be eradicated. So I've expanded my thoughts on the five blunders in *Living* and have added 22 more.

Included in this new list are some bumps in your approach to writing. The goal is to give you a better writing *life*, because it's not always easy. But you already know that. As David Eddings once put it, "Keep working. Keep trying. Keep believing. You still might not make it, but at least you gave it your best shot. If you don't have calluses on your soul, this isn't for you. Take up knitting instead."

I want this book to help you take your best shot and smooth out some of those calluses.

Let the ride begin.

1. Letting Fear Get a Foothold

All writers get the willies.

You don't get very far in the writing life without some shakes about your progress and prospects.

And no matter how much success you manage to achieve, there's always a part of you where fear tries to pitch a tent.

So what do you do?

The only thing you can do, and were meant to do: write your way out of it.

Emerson once said: *Do the thing you fear, and the death of fear is certain.*

Journal It

When fear steps in with a megaphone, sit down and write about it. Putting your fear on paper (or screen) is one way to lessen its power.

Start a journal. Identify the roots of your fear. So much of the time fear comes from what certain chuckleheads have told you over the years. Maybe when you were in school and that idiot teacher said you didn't have what it takes to be a writer, so you should probably consider taking shop.

Or maybe it was an early critique group you attended, and the Mussolini of the group told you how many rules you broke in that page you spent so much time on.

Maybe it's hearing all the stories about how hard it is to be a writer, how difficult it is to be "discovered," and, if discovered, break out.

Maybe you just are worried about starting on a journey that could very well lead you off a cliff.

Well here's the thing: there is no cliff. And even if there were, you would do as Ray Bradbury counseled—develop wings.

There is no failure in writing.

Unless you quit. Which you won't. Ever. (See blunder #25)

Keep Learning

Another thing you can do when fear hits is to go out and learn something.

I still find it exciting to build up my craft. There is no limitation on learning except that which you place upon yourself.

Maybe you fear you don't have the ability to write. If you know the English language well enough to hold a conversation with someone about more than what coffee to order at Starbucks, you have the ability to write.

Self Talk

Much of our fear is contained on an MP3 file in our head. It plays certain tracks over and over, like a favorites list of anxieties. Song titles such as:

I Told You You Can't Write
Who Are You Trying to Fool?
You'll Never Make It and You Can't Even Fake It

The Long and Winding Road is Too Doggone Hard
If I Only Had a Trust Fund

The thing about these tracks is that they're deeply planted. You can't really erase them, but you can override them—with self talk.

Turn up the volume on positive talk.

Write your own one liners.

Start with: *I can do this!*

Say that to yourself twelve times, emphasizing a different word each time.

I can do this!
I *can* do this!
I can *do* this!
I can do *this!*

Here's a little Neuro-linguistic programming (NLP) tip: Embed that self talk with a visual and a physical move.

The visual is something you dream up. It's a picture of yourself as a successful writer. What would that look like? Work on the picture until you *feel* it.

See your book listed as a #1 bestseller on Amazon.

See yourself on a panel of famous authors.

See an audience in rapt attention as you tell them about your latest book.

Got it? Now connect that feeling with a physical action. Something quick and definite. Like whapping your open palm with your fist (not so hard that it hurts!).

As you hit your palm, see that vision. Feel that feeling.

Practice that several times.

The next time you sit down to write, repeat the action. NLP recognizes that our physical and mental states are connected. The fist whap will bring back the feeling.

Which means you don't have to let your fears control you. You can knock them out proactively.

When it comes to fear, the only questions are: do you have the will to write, the desire to write, and the grit to stay with it? All that is a matter of decision. You *can* decide to be a writer, and no one else can tell you that you're not.

Write the thing you fear, and the death of fear is certain.

2. Putting Readers in the Tar Pits

Out here where I live, Los Angeles, we have a spot called the La Brea Tar Pits. My grandmother took me there when I was a boy. She told me that these big old dinosaurs would step into the pits and get stuck. The more they struggled, the faster they'd get sucked down.

I remember the smell of the hot tar as we stood outside the fence. I also remember not being able to shake this picture in my mind: What if I stuck my foot in the tar? Would that be the end of Jim? Would the entire Los Angeles Fire Department be unable to pull me out?

I think of the tar pits whenever I see opening pages in a manuscript that contain large amounts of exposition and back-story.

Exposition is material the author puts on the page to explain context.

Backstory is story material that happened in the past but for some authorial reason is dropped in the present.

When this kind of material appears as a "dump" in a scene, it slows the pace, sort of like a mastodon trying to run through the tar pits.

Before we go further, let me be clear that not all exposition and backstory is bad. In fact, properly handled, it's tremendously helpful for bonding reader with character.

But if it's plopped in large doses, and without a strategy in mind, it becomes a pool of hot goo where the story gets pitifully stuck.

Tar Removal Strategies

Do yourself a favor and highlight the exposition and backstory in your opening chapters and then cut all of it. Make a copy of the material, though. Look it over as a separate document.

Then put back in only what is necessary. And I do mean *necessary*. Be ruthless in deciding what a reader has to know, as opposed to what you *think* they have to know.

Quite often the writer has all this story info in his head and thinks the reader has to know most of it to understand what's going on. Not so! Readers get into story by way of characters facing challenge, conflict, change or trouble. If you give them that, they will wait a *long time* before wanting to know more whys and wherefores.

Next, see how much of this material you can put into dialogue. Dialogue is your best friend.

But make sure there is some form of tension or conflict in the dialogue. Why? Because straight exposition sounds phony coming out of a character's mouth:

> "Why Harry, it's so good to see you! I haven't seen you since we were kids back at Elmwood Elementary School in Bakersfield, remember? When I was just a shy girl who had recently moved from Minnesota, and you were the son of a Marine father and newspaper reporter mother?"

Ack.

Don't ever let readers catch you doing that. Instead, put information like this into real, conflicting dialogue that the characters would actually speak.

Arguments are especially good for exposition and backstory.

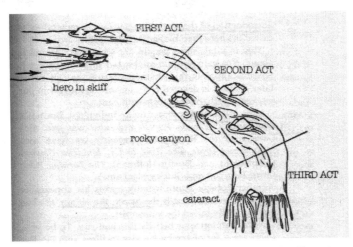

Recently I watched the Woody Allen film *Blue Jasmine,* and nodded approvingly at an early scene between Augie (Andrew Dice Clay) and his ex-wife, Ginger (Sally Hawkins). They're arguing about Ginger's sister, who calls herself Jasmine. A lot of background is revealed in this exchange:

"What's the rush, Ginger? You got a date?"

"It's none of your business. It happens to be Jeanette, so..."

"Jeanette?"

"Jasmine."

"What's she doing in town?"

"She's living with me till she gets back on her feet. She's had a bad time."

"When she had money, she wanted nothing to do with you. Now that she's broke, she's moving in."

"She's not just broke. She's screwed up. And it's none of your damn business. She's family."

"She stole our money."

"Okay!"

"Understand? We could have been set. That was our whole chance in life."

"For the last time, Augie, he was the crook, not her, okay? What the hell did she know about finance?"

"Don't stand there and tell me that. She's married to a guy for years, up to his ass in phony real estate and bank fraud. She knew nothing about it? Believe me, she knew, Ginger."

Another way to avoid the tar pits is this: *Act first, explain later.* Stamp this axiom on your writer's brain. Or put it on a note and tape it where you can see it. This advice never fails.

Start with something happening, an actual scene, before you even think about sprinkling in exposition.

Let's have a look at the opening of one of Robert B. Parker's Jesse Stone novels, *Stranger in Paradise:*

Molly Crane stuck her head in the doorway to Jesse's office.
"Man here to see you," she said. "Says his name's Wilson Cromartie."
Jesse looked up. His eyes met Molly's. Neither of them said anything. Then Jesse stood. His gun was in its holster on the file cabinet behind him. He took the gun from the holster and sat back down and put the gun in the top right-hand drawer of his desk and left the drawer open.
"Show him in," Jesse said.

As we will find out, Jesse Stone knows this Cromartie very well. He's called "Crow," and he's a Native American hit man. There is lots of backstory between Jesse and Crow. But Parker doesn't reveal any of it yet.

What he does instead is *show* Jesse getting his gun ready. That's intriguing. He knows something about this man after all, and it requires his gun being ready. Act first, explain later. The scene continues:

Molly went and in a moment returned with the man.
Jesse nodded his head.
"Crow," he said.
"Jesse Stone," Crow said.
Jesse pointed to a chair. Crow sat. He looked at the file cabinet.
"Empty holster," he said.
"Gun's in my desk drawer," Jesse said.
"And the drawer's open," Crow said.

"Uh-huh."

We now know that this Crow is someone who notices things, especially when it comes to guns. What kind of person is that? We don't know and Parker isn't telling us. We only know this guy is probably dangerous. This is not friendly small talk. The air is crackling with potential trouble.

Half a page later, we get this:

> "Last time I saw you was in a speedboat dashing off with a lot of money," Jesse said.
> "Long time back," Crow said. "Longer than the statute of limitations."
> "I'd have to check," Jesse said.
> "I did," Crow said. "Ten years."
> "Not for murder," Jesse said.
> "You got no evidence I had anything to do with murder."

Boom. Now we get backstory information, but notice where it is. In dialogue! And that, indeed, is how Parker delivers almost all the essential information in this novel.

Of course, Parker is writing in a particular, stripped-down style. But the principles he uses will serve you as well.

It may be your choice to render some backstory in narrative form. If you do, let me give you a rule of thumb (not the same as an unbreakable rule!) that I've given to many students with good results: in your first ten pages you can have three sentences of backstory, used all at once or spread out. In your second ten pages you can have three *paragraphs* of backstory, used all at once or spread out. But if you put backstory or exposition into dialogue, then you're free to use your own discretion. Just be sure the dialogue is truly what the characters would say and doesn't come off as a none-too-clever info dump. (I explain more about this in my book *How to Write Dazzling Dialogue.)*

Writing teachers spend a lot of time on sharp, intriguing openings. For good reason. That's what editors, agents, and browsing readers look at first. We don't want to leave them in the tar pits—we want them to keep on reading!

These tips will help keep you out of the goo.

Bonus: A Real World Critique

At my group blog, Kill Zone, we sometimes offer a critique of a first page, submitted anonymously. Below is one such submission. My notes are relevant to this discussion of tar pits. Used with the permission of the author, who was later revealed as novelist Terri Lynn Coop.

Ride the Lightning

I always knew my law degree would come in handy. I'd been promoted from bartender to manager of the strip club outside of Biloxi in less than three months. It hadn't hurt that the owner had walked in on my old boss auditioning a dancer on the couch in his office. The books were a mess, both sets. It turned out the staff wasn't all he'd been tapping.

Amateur.

No one would ever find the skim I'd set up. My dad had taught his only daughter well. The owner didn't have a problem with it because this time it all benefited him. As long as I kept the cash flowing, he gave me free rein to run The Lightning Lounge as I saw fit.

A definite management challenge cluttered my desk. I had to arrange the biggest bash in county history. The sheriff had commandeered the club for a party celebrating the execution of Billy Ray Draper. The former police officer, convicted of killing his wife, a Lightning Lounge dancer, was scheduled to get the stick in six weeks. The club owner told me to pull out all the stops and that the sky was the limit.

I riffled through my spreadsheets and made notes. The new sound system was online and the upgraded flooring gleamed and reflected the motion sensor lights. One huge problem remained. No matter how I shuffled the schedule, I didn't have enough waitresses and dancers to man the tables and the poles for the multi-day party. I'd placed ads and been interviewing, but the pickings were slim.

A knock at my office door interrupted my musing. Hopefully, part of the solution had just arrived.

"Come in."

She glided into the room on red stilettos. Her painted-on jeans and tank top hugged ample curves all the way up to a mass of blonde curls that Dolly Parton would kill for. She was no schoolgirl, the horizon of forty was clear in her face, but she owned it.

I took the out-stretched hand dripping with rings and jangly bracelets. Her grip was strong and sure. This was a woman who could wrestle trays of beer mugs and make it look easy.

My critique:

The first 3/4 of this page is all backstory, exposition and set-up. It's a common problem because writers think readers have to know certain information before the story can begin.

They don't.

Remember: *Act first, explain later.* Readers connect with characters in motion. They don't connect with exposition.

If you give readers an actual scene, with a disturbance thrown in, they will wait *a long time* before you need to explain anything to them.

Not only that, they don't need all your explanations at once, or in narrative form. I think it was Elmore Leonard who said that all the information a reader needs can be given in dialogue, and he's not far wrong.

So always start with something happening in the present moment. Later, if you decide you want to be stylish or poetic in the first paragraphs, that's up to you. Tremble when you do, though, and hear my voice in your head. *Act first, explain later.*

Here's a self-test. Check your opening pages for use of the word *had* and its derivatives. That's a dead giveaway that you're not in the present moment.

I'd
hadn't
had walked
he'd been tapping
My dad had taught
The Sheriff had

That's past tense. You don't want to open with the past. Oh, but doesn't *To Kill a Mockingbird* open that way? If you can write like Harper Lee and you want to go literary, have at it. But I still recommend the action way, even for literary types who would like to win a National Book Award before they die.

Look at your opening pages until you come to the place where an actual scene is happening. Or try the Chapter 2 Switcheroo, where you toss out Chapter 1 and make Chapter 2 the new beginning. That often works wonders.

Anyway, I'd start this novel here:

> She glided into the room on red stilettos. Her painted-on jeans and tank top hugged ample curves all the way up to a mass of blonde curls that Dolly Parton would kill for. She was no schoolgirl, the horizon of forty was clear in her face, but she owned it.
> I took the out-stretched hand dripping with rings and jangly bracelets. Her grip was strong and sure. This was a woman who could wrestle trays of beer mugs and make it look easy.

A couple of suggestions. Always check your pop culture references to make sure they're not too dated. I hope I'm not insulting Dolly Parton, but is she that well-known anymore to people under 40? I've been editing my WIP and saw that I'd referenced a hit song from the 1980s. Oops. I did a little research and found a hit song from 2005 that worked much better.

Even so, be selective with these things, because in a few years they may become terribly awkward. How about all those books published before 1995 that used favorable O. J. Simpson references?

Now to some micro-editing:

She was no schoolgirl, the horizon of forty was clear in her face, but she owned it.

Here is where our good friends *Show, don't tell* and *Don't gild the lily* come in. That first clause is a *tell*. And it is not necessary, because the rest of the line does the work and does it well:

The horizon of forty was clear in her face, but she owned it.

Isn't that crisper? You want that standing alone, not fuzzed up with a *tell* before or after. I see this all the time. Things like: *I ran up the hill. My lungs were on fire. Sweat flopped off my forehead. I was dog tired.*

That last sentence adds nothing. In fact, it takes something away from the immediate experience by the reader. It's a little "speed bump." Too many of these and the ride is ruined.

Let's look at this sentence now:

I took the out-stretched hand dripping with rings and jangly bracelets.

I like the use of sight and sound here. But a tiny speed bump as I was wondering how jangly bracelets were dripping from her *hand.* It's not too bad because know what the author meant to convey. Still, I'd consider making it clearer. Something like:

Bracelets jangled as she stretched out a hand studded with rings.

Finally:

This was a woman who could wrestle trays of beer mugs and make it look easy.

I know what the author means, but *wrestling* seems much different than *carrying.* In my own writing, the things I always find during revision are metaphors and word pictures that don't quite make it. That's when I hunker down and try to figure out a way to make them work or simply come up with something else.

I advise the writer to tweak this one, and also to

brainstorm a few other word pictures. Then choose the one that works best.

All that being said, I am interested in this character who slid into the room in stilettos. And I'd love to see the next few lines be dialogue that begin to give us a picture of the narrator and where she works, and so on.

3. Marshmallow Dialogue

"Hello, Becky."

"Hi, Kelly."

"So, how is everything at home?"

"Oh, you know, the same."

"I do! I totally know about that. It's like that at my house, too!"

"Really?"

"Really."

"It's good to know I'm not alone."

"Yes it is. Awfully good."

"Well, listen, I've got something to tell you."

"Really? I'm all ears."

Unfortunately, at this point the readers are not all ears. If they're not asleep, they are wondering why they are bothering with this story.

Dialogue without conflict or tension is squishy and sweet. Like a marshmallow.

Marshmallows are for hot chocolate and S'Mores, not fiction.

Let's take a quick look at the above confection.

First, there is no sign of trouble anywhere in these lines. This is the kind of talk that goes on every day in countless coffee houses and kitchens, bus benches and laundromats. It's the talk that comes out of people without any care or worry at the moment of speaking.

Or, if they are worried, are good at hiding it.

Which is precisely the kind of talk we don't want in our stories.

We want care. And worry. And we want to see it, or at least sense it.

Notice, too, how the above dialogue gets bogged down with needless wordage. *So, Oh, Well, listen, Really? Really. Really?*

This is a blunder because trouble is what binds the reader to a story. They first get worried when a character faces change or challenge. They want to worry about the character for the rest of the book. If dialogue doesn't have tension or conflict, the reader gets a little more detached.

Attitudes and Agendas

Make sure every character in your book, from the majors to the minors, have both an attitude and an agenda.

A character's attitude is the product of backstory. Therefore, you must know at least the bare minimum of where your characters are from, what their education is like, what words they are likely to use.

The tool I like best for getting to know a character is the voice journal. This is a free form document, written in the character's own voice. I prod the character with questions and let him speak. I keep this document going until the voice is unique. For a major character this document may be several pages. For a minor character, it's probably going to be less than a page.

After attitude comes agenda. Every character in your story should want something. In every scene, too, the characters will have objectives. Even if, as Kurt Vonnegut once suggested, it's only a glass of water. Then you figure out ways to have the characters manifest their different agendas in the dialogue.

Tension and Fear

Then there is tension. Tension might not be a matter of two characters in complete opposition to one another. It can be whatever is putting a strain on conversation. That can be one character's refusal to be open and honest, or it might simply be something inside one of the characters that makes communication difficult.

One of the best things a character can have, from an author's point of view, is fear. Fear is a continuum. It goes from simple worry to outright terror. But in every story where the stakes are high, one character in every scene—the point of view character, usually the Lead—will be worried about something, fearful about what's happening, afraid of what might happen, or of being found out.

So one very simple way to avoid marshmallow dialogue is to ask yourself where the conflict, tension, or fear is coming from.

Finally, tighten all the dialogue. Look for those mushy words that come at the beginning of sentences. Don't have characters echo what other characters say, unless there's a reason for it.

Mix in reactions with your dialogue. Use inner thoughts and feelings to reveal the tense emotional content below the surface of the words.

Don't forget silences, too.

Let us return, then, to the dialogue that opened this chapter. How are Becky and Kelly doing now?

> "Hello, Becky," Kelly said.
> Becky said nothing.
> "How's everything at home?"
> "Same," Becky said.
> "It's like that at my house, too!"
> "Well La-Dee-Dah."
> "I mean—"
> "I know what you mean."
> Kelly put her hand on her chest. "But I've got something to tell you."
> Tell it in hell.

4. Generic Description

Catnip makes cats happy. Super happy. Dreamlike happy. They forget they are cats and think they are lions with wings. It's a drug-induced, feline high. There's an oil in catnip called *nepetalactone*, and when smelled by Fluffy it activates neurons that signal a "far out, man" response in cats.

The subtle yet specific smell transports them.

Well, subtle and specific details are catnip for the reader's mind. They transport, create a momentary high. Because the right details place the reader into a scene in an experiential way.

I say subtle, because overbearing description pulls the readers out of a book. It is a writer trying too hard. It's a rubber hammer to the head instead of a nice, soothing back rub.

One subtle, specific detail is worth a thousand words of generic description. In scene moments of high emotion, for example, look for that one image that evokes the inner life of the character and the essence of the scene.

In Ernest Hemingway's short story "Soldiers Home" there is a famous detail that, for me, captures the entire mood of the story. A young man, Krebs, returning from World War

I, has come home. But he's not the same. Something has gone out of him. He doesn't do much around the house or anywhere else.

In one scene, his mother has just served him breakfast. You get the feeling the mother is trying too hard to make things normal. It's started to get to Krebs.

His mother starts going on and on about how worried she is about him. About how he doesn't seem to have any ambition and so on. As she speaks, her son says nothing. At one point Hemingway writes:

Krebs looked at the bacon fat hardening on his plate.

That detail helps us *feel* what Krebs is feeling. We don't need Hemingway *telling* us how he felt.

That's what a telling detail is.

These days, there is a minimalist preference in description. Less is more.

Descriptions should also be filtered through the viewpoint character. You don't want to be general when you can enhance tone and feeling.

Here's an example from one of the great paperback original writers of the 60s and 70s, Marvin Albert. He wrote several detective novels as Anthony Rome, who was also the narrator and hero of the books.

In *Miami Mayhem,* a wealthy woman lets Tony Rome into her large Miami Beach home:

She led the way through a wide entry hall with a marble-tile floor and pecky-cypress walls covered with huge abstract paintings. Her walk was graceful, with controlled strength to it.

I followed her past a living room about the size of a luxury-hotel lobby, gold-and-brown dining area almost the same size, a kitchen large and gleaming enough to accommodate twenty ice skaters.

That's in keeping with the first-person narrator's voice.

More Tips

• Taste, smell, and touch are underused sensory details. Every now and then weave one of these onto a page.

• Remember that less is more, if the less is really sharp. Another way of saying this is "don't gild the lily." That old expression means refrain from adding something when what is already there is doing the job.

With description and detail, the one that illuminates most is the one that should stand alone. A common mistake is to describe and then *tell* what the description means. Such as:

The rain fell outside, hitting the empty trash cans on the side of the house. He felt lonely.

I dropped my books in front of everybody. The stares were like high beams of onrushing cars.
How embarrassing.

We don't need the author to *tell* us what the character is feeling. The descriptions do the job.

• Don't stress about the details during a first draft. Do the best you can, give them some thought, but push on with the story. The best time to come up with telling details and just the right image is during revision. Give yourself time to do this. It's worth it. Because the readers are going to love that catnip. It's going to make them think and feel that your books are a cut above the average.

• If I were to recommend one book on this subject, it would be *Description* by Monica Wood, published by Writer's Digest Books.

5. Pure Evil Villains

Back when I was pounding the Off-Broadway boards I got a small part in a production of *Othello*. Our lead was the marvelous stage actor Earle Hyman, better known to most of you as Bill Cosby's father on *The Cosby Show*. In point of fact Earle is one of the great Othellos. He is also a very nice man.

Once we were chatting backstage and I told him that someday I would love to play Iago. He said I would be perfect for it because I had such an open, honest face (this was before I went to law school). That, after all, is what makes Iago powerful. Othello calls him "My friend, honest, honest Iago." And if the part is played right there is even a touch of sympathy for Iago at the end as he's dragged off to be tortured to death.

This, in fact, is what set Shakespeare apart from his contemporaries. He knew how to mangle the emotions of the audience, even to the point of rendering some sympathy for the devil.

Dean Koontz wrote, "The best villains are those that evoke pity and sometimes even genuine sympathy as well as terror. Think of the pathetic aspect of the Frankenstein monster. Think of the poor werewolf, hating what he becomes in the light of the full moon, but incapable of resisting the lycan-thropic tides in his own cells."

All this to say that the best villains in fiction, theatre, and film are never one-dimensional. They are complex, often charming, and able to manipulate. The biggest mistake you can make with a villain is to make him pure evil or all crazy.

Not every antagonist is a villain, of course. In *The Fugitive*, Sam Gerard (Tommy Lee Jones) is a lawman. He just has the job of catching Dr. Richard Kimble (Harrison Ford).

But when you have a true villain, make sure you do three things.

1. Give him an argument

There is only one character in all storytelling who wakes up each day asking himself what fresh evil he can commit. This guy:

But other than Dr. Evil, every villain feels justified in what he is doing. When you make that clear to the reader in a way that approaches actual empathy, you will create cross-currents of emotion that deepen the fictive dream like virtually nothing else.

One of the techniques I teach in my workshops is borrowed

from my courtroom days. I ask people to imagine their villain has been put on trial and is representing himself. Now comes the time for the closing argument. He has one opportunity to make his case for the jury. He has to justify his whole life. He has to appeal to the jurors' hearts and minds or he's doomed.

Write that speech. Do it as a free-form document, in the villain's voice, with all the emotion you can muster. Emphasize what's called "exculpatory evidence." That is evidence that, if believed, would tend to exonerate a defendant. As the saying goes, give the devil his due.

Note: This does not mean you are giving approval to what the villain has done. No way. What you are getting at is his motivation. This is how to know what's going on inside your villain's head throughout the entire novel.

Want to read a real-world example? See the cross-examination of Hermann Goering from the Nuremberg Trials. Here's a clip:

> I think you did not quite understand me correctly here, for I did not put it that way at all. I stated that it had struck me that Hitler had very definite views of the impotency of protest; secondly, that he was of the opinion that Germany must be freed from the dictate of Versailles. It was not only Adolf Hitler; every German, every patriotic German had the same feelings. And I, being an ardent patriot, bitterly felt the shame of the dictate of Versailles, and I allied myself with the man about whom I felt perceived most clearly the consequences of this dictate, and that probably he was the man who would find the ways and means to set it aside. All the other talk in the Party about Versailles was, pardon the expression, mere twaddle ... From the beginning it was the aim of Adolf Hitler and his movement to free Germany from the oppressive fetters of Versailles, that is, not from the whole Treaty of Versailles, but from those terms which were strangling Germany's future.

How chilling to hear a Nazi thug making a reasoned argument to justify the horrors foisted upon the world by Hitler. So much scarier than a cardboard bad guy.

So what's your villain's justification? Let's hear it.

Marshal the evidence. Know deeply and intimately what drives him.

2. Choices

It's common and perhaps a little trite these days to give the villain a horrific backstory and leave it at that.

Or, contrarily, to leave out any backstory at all.

In truth, everyone alive or fictional has a backstory, and you need to know your villain's. But don't just make him a victim of abuse. Make him a victim of his own choices.

Back when virtue and character were actually taught to children in school, there was a lesson from the *McGuffey Reader* that went like this: "The boy who will peep into a drawer will be tempted to take something out of it; and he who will steal a penny in his youth will steal a pound in his manhood."

The message, of course, is that *we are responsible for our choices and actions, and they have consequences.*

In *Mere Christianity* C. S. Lewis wrote:

> Good and evil both increase at compound interest. That is why the little decisions you and I make every day are of such infinite importance. The smallest good act today is the capture of a strategic point from which, a few months later, you may be able to go on to victories you never dreamed of. An apparently trivial indulgence in lust or anger today is the loss of a ridge or railway line or bridgehead from which the enemy may launch an attack otherwise impossible.

So what was the first choice your villain made that began forging his long chain of depravity? Write that scene. Give us the emotion of it. Even if you don't use the scene in your book, knowing it will give your villain scope.

3. Attractiveness

The devil is not a cloven-hoofed, red-suited, pointy-eared demon with a pitchfork. Indeed, the Bible says Satan appears "as an angel of light." He is the most beautiful of the heavenly host. His mode is to entice, not coerce.

The same with the best villains. They are sometimes attractive through raw, worldly power (Gordon Gekko). Intellect may be their weapon (Hannibal Lecter). Or a certain way with the opposite sex (innumerable *homme* and *femme fatales*). Hitchcock's best villains were charming and therefore disarming. They often had wit and style. (My favorite is the widow-murdering uncle played by Joseph Cotten in *Shadow of a Doubt.)*

Give your villain at least one attractive feature and then see what the other characters do with it.

If you create a three-dimensional villain, and add a touch of empathy as well, you'll have your storytelling hooks deeply embedded in the readers' hearts.

6. The Expected

Somerset Maugham, the famous English novelist, once said, "There are three rules for writing the novel. Unfortunately, no one knows what they are."

That's been quoted a lot, though I have to disagree with old Maugham. There are some rules, though a writer may choose to break them if he so chooses. (Some people don't like the idea of "rules" in an art form. Okay. Fine. Call these things the *things that work.*)

There is at least one rule, however, that no writer should break. Ever. Unless you are content to sit alone at Starbucks writing only for yourself.

That rule is: *Don't bore the reader.*

It therefore behooves us (good word, *behooves)* to consider the question of what boring is.

Can we not simply say it is the mundane and the *expected?*

That's the way it is in our lives. When we are going through a routine and we know what it's going to be and how it is going to turn out, and it does turn out that way, we experience boredom. No surprise. No spice.

So try this:

Pause every now and then and think about your plot. Ask yourself what would the reader expect to happen next? What are the stereotypical story tropes that immediately spring to your mind? Maybe you've already mapped out your plot and it seems a little predictable to you.

Take your time. Then ponder the list. All you have to do is take the most obvious turns and do something different, something opposite.

Try this with characters, too. Have the character do something the very opposite of what you and the readers would expect that character to do. Go crazy with this. Try things. And when something hits you that is pleasing, justify it. Let the thing happen then justify it later.

When writing a scene, I always try to put in something unexpected. This can be as big as a new character coming in. It's like the old Raymond Chandler advice, when things get dull just bring in a guy with a gun. It doesn't have to be a gun, but it can be a new character who has trouble to offer.

Or you can go small, with a line of dialogue that is so unexpected it would cause the reader to sit up and take notice.

A fun little exercise I do sometimes is to go grab a novel off the shelf, open it at random and find the first line of dialogue on the page. Then I stick that line of dialogue right in the middle of the scene. Sometimes the line will suggest another line of dialogue. It will make me think that the character says something so strange but I'll think about it, justify it, and put it in.

Try the dictionary game, too. I carry a little pocket dictionary when I go somewhere to write. Every so often I'll stop in a scene and pop open the dictionary at random. I put my finger on a page and then scan for the first noun I see. Then I let the noun suggest something for my writing.

So let's say I'm writing a tense scene between a husband and wife, where the wife has just found evidence of infidelity. They're in their apartment, and she holds up some lacy underwear and asks him where it came from.

He begins to think up a story.

What kind of story?

I open the dictionary, and find this word: *haddock*.

My mind starts churning:

Fish. He was out at a fish place. Or he had gone fishing. And his buddy played a joke on him by putting a pair of his girlfriend's panties in his fishing box, and when he got home there they were, and he meant to throw them out. That could be his story.

Or he could say, "I know this looks fishy."

Or he could flop his arms around. They look like fish flopping on a deck.

I sort of like the last one. It's a description I never would have come up with without the dictionary's help.

7. Low Stakes

I've read a number of manuscripts over the years about cops and detectives who get a horrendous case—serial killer, serial rapist, graphic murder—that starts off with a bang and rapidly becomes a yawn.

This, even though there are scenes of violence, tension, conflict, and snappy dialogue.

It feels like something's missing.

There is.

Death.

No, not the deaths of the victims. It's the professional or psychological death of the cop—it's not on the line.

What I mean is that the author has not made it clear to the reader that this particular case is a matter of the cop losing his job or his soul. He's doing his job, sure. But the job itself is not on the line, nor is his ability to function as a human being on the chopping block.

I teach that a great story is about a character's fight with death. It can be physical death, as in thrillers. A bad guy is trying to kill the good guy.

But in other books the death can be professional or psychological.

It needs to be one of these three, or some combination of them all.

In the Harry Bosch books by Michael Connelly, it's clear that Bosch *must* be a voice for the voiceless, a seeker of justice for the victims. Every case is personal to him. There is an aspect of psychological death on the line.

A detective could have his job in jeopardy. If he doesn't solve this crime, he'll be demoted and chained to a desk.

A criminal defense lawyer gets a case. It shouldn't just be about the case. It needs to be personal to the lawyer, so important that to lose it would forever scar him. Or at the very least, ruin his reputation (professional death).

You, writer, have to find that death element and *show* the Lead experiencing that realization.

There's a moment in the Paul Newman film, *The Verdict*, where the bottom-feeding, alcoholic lawyer is in the hospital, taking a picture of the comatose victim he representing. To this point the case was going to be another of his quick settlements.

But looking at the poor woman, hooked up to life support because of the hospital's negligence, his face changes. A nurse comes in and says, "You can't be here."

Newman keeps looking at the woman and quietly says, "I'm her attorney."

It's his realization that this is his last shot at being a real lawyer, one who cares about his client more than quick bucks.

If he fails this time—as he has so many times in the recent past—it's going to be all over for him, both professionally and psychologically.

All with the one line.

You can do the same in your fiction. You can create a moment that shows us just how high the stakes are for the Lead character.

Do it.

Then create several more moments that intensify the death stakes, and weave them into the plot.

8. Fumbled Flashbacks

A lot of writing teachers warn about flashbacks. Some simply echo Sinclair Lewis who, when asked how best to handle flashbacks, said, "Don't."

That's a bit extreme. Many novelists successfully utilize flashbacks. You can, too, if you handle them with great care.

The first question to ask about a flashback scene is, *Is it necessary?* Be firm about this. Does the story information have to come to us in this fashion?

A flashback is almost always used to explain why characters act a certain way in the present story. If such information can be dropped in during a present moment scene, that's usually the better choice.

And be wary of starting your novel in the present and going too soon to flashback. If the flashback is important, you should consider starting with that scene as a prologue or first chapter.

These are guidelines. In the hands of a good writer, a gripping first chapter, followed by a compelling flashback, can work--see the first two chapters of Lee Child's *Persuader* for an example.

If you've decided that a flashback is necessary, make sure it works *as a scene*—immediate, confrontational. Write it as a unit of dramatic action, and not as an information dump. Not:

> Jack remembered when he was a child, and he spilled the gasoline on the ground. His father got so angry at him it scared Jack. His father hit him, and yelled at him. It was something Jack would never forget . . . [and more of the same]

Instead:

> Jack couldn't help remembering the gas can. He was eight, and all he wanted to do was play with it.
> The garage was his theater. No one was home. He held the can aloft, like the hammer of Thor. "I am the king of gas!" he said. "I will set you all on fire!"
> Jack stared down at the imaginary humans below his feet
> The gas can slipped from his hand.
> Unable to catch it, Jack watched as the can made a horrible thunking sound. Its contents poured out on the new concrete.
> Jack quickly righted the can, but it was too late. A big, smelly puddle was right in the middle of the garage.
> *Dad is going to kill me!*
> Jack looked around for a rag, anything to clean up the mess.
> He heard the garage door open.
> And saw his dad's car pull into the driveway.

A well written flashback scene will not detract from your story. Readers are used to novels cutting away from one scene to another. They will accept a cut to a flashback if it is written with dramatic flair.

How do you get in and out of a flashback, so it flows naturally? Here's one way that works every time.

In the scene you're writing, when you're about to go to flashback, put in a strong, sensory detail that triggers the memory in the point-of-view character:

Wendy looked at the wall and saw an ugly, black spider making its way up toward a web where a fly struggled. Legs creeping, moving slowly toward its prey. The way Lester had moved on Wendy all those years ago.

She was sixteen and Lester was the big man on campus. "Hey," he called to her one day by the lockers. "You want to go see a movie?"

We are in the flashback. Now write it out as a dramatic scene.

How do we get out of it?

By returning to the sensory detail:

Lester made his move in the back of the car. Wendy was helpless. It was all over in five minutes.

The spider was at the web now. Waves of nausea washed over Wendy as she watched. But she could not look away.

Watch out for the word *had* in your flashback scenes. Use one or two to get in, but once in, they are mostly unnecessary. Instead of:

Marvin had been good at basketball. He had tried out for the team, and the coach had said how good he was.

"I think I'll make you my starting point guard," Coach had told him right after try outs.

Marvin had been thrilled by that.

Do this:

Marvin had been good at basketball. He tried out for the team, and the coach said how good he was.

"I think I'll make you my starting point guard," Coach told him right after try outs.

Marvin was thrilled.

Flashback scene alternatives

An alternative to the flashback scene (which you may be

tempted to turn into an information dump) is the *back flash*. These are short bursts in which you drop information about the past within a present moment scene. The two primary methods are *dialogue* and *thoughts*.

DIALOGUE

"Hey, don't I know you?"

"No."

"Yeah, yeah. You were in the newspapers, what, ten years ago? The kid who killed his parents in that cabin."

"You're wrong."

"Chester A. Arthur! You were named after the president. I remember that in the story."

Chester's troubled background has come out in a flash of dialogue. This is also a good way for shocking information from the past, or a dark secret, to be revealed at a tense moment in the story.

THOUGHTS

"Hey, don't I know you?"

"No." Did he? Did the guy recognize him? Would everybody in town find out he was Chet Arthur, killer of parents?

"Yeah, yeah. You were in the newspapers, what, ten years ago?"

It was twelve years ago, and this guy had him pegged. Lousy press, saying he killed his parents because he was high on drugs. They didn't care about the abuse, did they? And this guy wouldn't, either.

We are in Chester's head for this one, as he reflects on his past. If you want to do a full flashback scene, thoughts can also operate as a transition point.

The skillful handling of flashback material is one mark of a good writer. Using back flashes as an alternative is usually the mark of a wise writer.

9. Neglected Brain

It's a major blunder to ignore your brain. If you take it for granted it may go on strike, or take an extended vacation with all your files.

Don't let that happen.

Nurturing and unloosing your brain are critical to your success as a writer. Take care of the gray matter and it will take care of your stories.

So let's talk about two aspects of the brain: its health and its freedom.

Brain Health

Things we know that are good for the brain:

Foods

Salmon, blueberries, tomatoes, walnuts, red wine (in moderation), green tea, avocados, eggs (in moderation), kale (if you can figure out a way to eat it that won't make you feel like you're imprisoned at a Big Sur health compound). Moderate intake of coffee and wine, if you're of a mind (to coin a phrase).

Sleep

Eight hours if you're very young.
>   Seven hours if you're under fifty.
>   Six hours after that.
>   Power naps helps overcome lack of sleep. You can train yourself to nod off for 20 minutes, and then wake up refreshed.
>   If napping doesn't work for you, try this: find a quiet place where you can lie on your back with your legs on a chair. Relax and deep breathe for 10-15 minutes.

Strengthening exercises

Crossword puzzles, sudoku, doing things with your opposite hand (like brushing your teeth or shaving, but not handling firearms or defusing incendiary devices), memorization tricks, reading challenging material for at least ten minutes and jotting notes about what it means. A moderate use of video games.

Atmosphere

Research is beginning to mount that low lighting and some ambient noise are ideal for the creative part of the brain. Writing in a coffee joint is good, but you can recreate that environment in your own home.
>   Lower the lights.
>   Tune into Coffitivity.com and select your preferred coffeehouse level.
>   Rain sounds are nice, too. Check out Jazzandrain.com.
>   Go wherever you like...by which I mean set up a background on your computer. I write with Scrivener, the hugely popular app, and one of my favorite features is the Composition mode that allows you to put up a photo and your document. I love the famous L.A. deli, Langer's, so that's my "writing space."

I know people are sometimes intimidated by Scrivener, so I've included a Bonus section on how to start using it without fear.

Brain Set Free

Interesting research indicates that individual brainstorming may actually be more effective than a group session. From an article from Medium.com:

> Researchers in Minnesota tested this with scientists and advertising executives from the 3M Company. Half the subjects worked in groups of four. The other half worked alone, and then their results were randomly combined as if they had worked in a group, with duplicate ideas counted only once. In every case, four people working individually generated between 30 to 40 percent more ideas than four people working in a group. Their results were of a higher quality, too: independent judges assessed the work and found that the individuals produced better ideas than the groups.
>
> Follow-up research tested whether larger groups performed any better. In one study, 168 people were either divided into teams of five, seven, or nine or asked to work individually. The research confirmed that working individually is more productive than working in groups. It also

showed that productivity decreases as group size increases. The conclusion: "Group brainstorming, over a wide range of group sizes, inhibits rather than facilitates creative thinking." The groups produced fewer and worse results because they were more likely to get fixated on one idea and because, despite all exhortations to the contrary, some members felt inhibited and refrained from full participation.

I advocate a weekly creativity time. One half hour at least. This is when you are going to go someplace other than your normal work station and just play in the fields of your mind.

My usual practice is to head for a Starbucks or Coffee Bean and score a soft chair.

I take a notebook, pen, earbuds.

I leave my laptop at home.

And I play games. Such as:

The First Line Game: Make up killer first lines. One after another. I once came up with this and really want to write a story around it:

I was doing about eighty, with Samuel Cornell's left leg thumping around in my trunk, when I saw the cop car in my rear view mirror.

I have a whole file of first lines. It's a great workout for the brain and I'll never lack for something to write about.

The Title Game: Make up a bunch of titles, too.

The Killer Scene Game: Just start imagining great scenes. See them in your mind and justify them later. Who are these people? Why are they doing what they're doing? What's happening beneath the surface?

Noodling the Newspaper: For this I like an old-fashioned paper, fished out from the used news rack at Starbucks, or on occasion I'll plunk down the money. I go through each story, read the headline and the first half, then create a story out of it. I circle things with a pen. I make doodles.

Who Are They? This game is simple observation. I look at people. I try to create a backstory for them. I put in some what ifs.

You can come up with your own games, but the point is to play. Get your brain frolicking and it will get stronger and happier. Then when you're working on a project, it's a healthy partner for you to have.

10. Happy People in Happy Land

Great works of fiction are not about happy people living in Happy Land. They are about people being snatched from Happy Land and thrust into a dark world, where they can never rest until they face down a death threat.

Over the years I've seen innumerable manuscripts that have a HPIHL opening chapter. The mother fixing her ideal family breakfast. The Boston debutante getting ready to leave on a ship bound for England. The child—who will become a hero—playing a game contentedly in his room while the author pours out all the setting and backstory.

The reason this happens is that the author thinks the reader has to get to know these nice people up front, so when trouble finally arrives the reader will be invested in them, not wanting to see such nice people in trouble!

But by the time that trouble comes, the reader may have put down the book.

Readers do not care about happy people in Happy Land.

On the other hand, if they see a character facing a disturbing opening situation, they will follow that character a long time before needing to know more about them.

One of my axioms is: *act first, explain later.* Have the characters in motion toward something, and fill in the details of the situation a little at a time, and only after the action is established.

Begin your novel not with a happy setting, but with a *disturbance to* the setting. Something that is *different* in the character's "ordinary world." Portent, change, shift, challenge, trouble, danger, another character.

A disturbance can be relatively quiet, or big and "action-y."

An email or a monster.

A doorbell or a gunshot.

Just so long as it causes a ripple or a splash in the pool of the character's life.

I've seen a number of manuscripts that are about a happy *person* waking up in Happy Land. "Character alone, thinking" scenes are usually not fraught with trouble. Suppose you wrote this:

> The sun rose bright over the bay. Andie stretched and got out of bed, and looked out the window. The pelicans were already cruising for their breakfast.
>
> Ah, breakfast! Her very first here in Wonderful, Massachusetts. She'd come to this little town that she and Frank had fallen in love with so many years ago.
>
> This would be the place where she would start over.
>
> This would be the place she would begin to paint again.
>
> Throwing on a robe, Andie went into the bathroom and looked at herself in the mirror. She moved a tuft of her auburn hair over her left ear, making her green eyes all the more visible to her, eyes that her mother always said held the promise of great things.
>
> "Your eyes hold the promise of great things," her mother always said.

What do you do when your crit partner tells you she's not interested in Andie in the least?

One strategy is to read through your pages until you get to a place where there is another character present, and dialogue is possible. Start there.

The bell over the bun shop door jangled merrily as Andie stepped in from the cool, morning street.

"Hello, Millie," Andie said.

"Hello, Andie," Millie said from behind the counter. She was a sixty-year-old widow who'd started Buns o' Fun when her husband of thirty years, Herman, died. Since the bun shop had opened it had done a brisk business for the locals and tourists alike.

"The usual?" Millie asked in her sing-song voice.

"You bet!" said Andie.

Well, we're a little better off, but there is still no disturbance. Keep looking in your manuscript for the first sign of change, challenge, or trouble. Or make it up now and put it at the beginning.

The bell over the bun shop door jammed as Andie Magruder stepped in from the cool, morning street.

"Something wrong with the bell, Millie," Andie said.

Millie, the sixty-year-old owner of Buns o' Fun, said nothing from behind the counter.

"You want me to call Heck Suling to come fix it?" Andie said.

"I'm so sorry," Millie said.

"Sorry? What for?"

"You mean you haven't heard?"

"Heard what?"

Millie looked down, wiped her hands on her apron.

Avoiding HPIHL is also essential at every stage of your novel. With the action well underway, and death stakes on the line, there needs to be a cloud of fear or dread over the proceedings.

Now, this does not mean that you can't have a quiet scene, even a happy one, for a change of pace in the story—so long as the reader is aware that this happiness is temporary.

In *The Wizard of Oz*, Dorothy, the Scarecrow, and the Tin Man are walking through the dark forest, full of "lions, and tigers, and bears, oh my!" Happiness is on hold.

Then they are "attacked" by the Cowardly Lion. There's a confrontation, Dorothy slaps his nose, and he starts crying.

He admits his cowardice and sings a little song about it. He's invited to join them on the trip to see the Wizard, and there follows a scene of optimism and skipping down the yellow-brick road. They are off to see the Wizard!

But then the film pulls back to let us see the Wicked Witch watching the whole thing. And we know the happiness is not going to last.

A good way to think about happiness in a novel is that it is not a Land, a dwelling place, or a safe locale. It is the ultimate destination, the place the Lead wants to get to—or get back to.

Don't think that you have to eschew any relatively peaceful scene in your novel. It's a good thing to give the reader a little breathing space.

But when you do, follow these two guidelines.

1. Make the scene relatively short. If the happiness goes on too long, there will be unhappy people out there called *readers*.

2. Apply equal and opposite *unhappiness*. That is, if the scene seems to bring massive happiness or relief to the characters, hammer them with an occurrence of equally massive unhappiness or danger directly afterward. If it's a bit of happiness, weave in a bit of dread.

11. Head Hopping

Head hopping is the way some editors refer to a point of view mistake. The prevailing wisdom in fiction is that each scene should have only one POV. So if it's a romance between Don and Dora, and we get what Don thinks and feels, we're "inside Don's head." We see everything in the scene through his senses. Or should.

If we suddenly switch over to Dora's thoughts, we have hopped heads, like an alien looking for a new host. The theory is that this sudden shift removes some of the intimacy that's been established with Don.

Here's what I mean. See if you can spot the hop:

> Don gazed into Dora's eyes. They were deep blue, like the roiling sea. He found himself getting lost in her look.
> Stop it! You'll look like a fool.
> "What's that after shave you're wearing?" Dora said.
> "Hm?" Don kept his voice low, non-committal.
> "That smell." It was intoxicating. "I love it."
> "It's called Hai Karate," Don said. "It was big in the 1960s. I just uncovered a stash of it in my grandfather's garage."

> He wanted to take her hand, but hesitated. His brown eyes seemed to darken a bit.

So where was the first hop? We start off seeing and feeling inside Don's head. Then all of a sudden we get those three words, It was intoxicating. Coming between Dora's two lines of dialogue, that has to be something Dora is feeling.

We go back to Don's POV until the last line. Why is that a head hop? Because Don is not looking at his own eyes, let alone observing them darken. That has to be coming from Dora's POV, because she is the only one to whom it can *seem* Don's eyes are darkening.

Now, let me be perfectly frank and Victorian. There is nothing illegal about head hopping. It used to be done all the time, especially when novels were written in what we call Omniscient POV, where the writer is free to hop around, or limit himself, as he wishes.

Technically, it's okay. It's just that over time fictional style has become more emotion oriented, and that means the intimacy I spoke of earlier is best established by sticking to one POV for a scene, or even a whole book.

The rule of thumb is, one POV per scene, a close POV, either First person (I went into the store) or 3d person (He went into the store).

If you want to switch over to another character's POV, you can start a new chapter or do a white-space break and start up again. Thus:

> Don gazed into Dora's eyes. They were deep blue, like the roiling sea. He found himself getting lost in her look.
> Stop it! You'll look like a fool.
> "What's that after shave you're wearing?" Dora said.
> "Hm?" Don kept his voice low, non-committal.
> "That smell. I love it."
> "It's called Hai Karate," Don said. "It was big in the 1960s. I just uncovered a stash of it in my grandfather's garage."
> He wanted to take her hand, but hesitated.
> Sam "The Hitman" Simms munched a breadstick and

watched the soon-to-be-dead couple on the other side of the restaurant.

Too bad, he thought. Just when they're getting to know each other.

That's a jump within the same scene. Perfectly all right. It just depends on your strategy.

So how do you avoid head hopping?

You just have to learn by experience.

One way is to have a good freelance editor go over your manuscript with explicit instructions to look for POV lapses.

You can try this yourself, too. Highlight every sense perception and thought in a scene, then see if they are properly placed.

One recurring problem area is facial expressions. Remember, a character cannot see her own expression unless she's looking in a mirror or a very shiny toaster!

12. Point of View Confusion

Even veteran writers sometimes get in a fog about Point of View.

I'd like to approach the subject in a little different manner than most. Before getting into the differences, let's talk about the *effects*.

There is a range of intimacy in POV. The most intimate is First Person, where the narration is coming from the head and heart of the character. We get the closest possible connection to the thoughts and feelings of the Lead.

By way of contrast, the omniscient POV is the least intimate. While the omniscient narrator can roam freely and go into any character's head, that very freedom prevents the close focus on one character.

Between First Person and Omniscient is Third Person, which comes in two forms—Limited and Unlimited. Limited means you stick with one character throughout the book. You don't stray into the perceptions of any other character. Done well, this can become almost as intimate as First Person.

Unlimited means you can switch POV to another character in another scene.

By they way, I'm not even going to mention Second Person POV, which is as rare as the blue-footed booby. Second Person sounds like this:

> You walk into the party, like you are walking onto a yacht. Your hat is strategically tipped below one eye. You see Carly Simon glaring at you from across the room.

My advice is not to try Second Person, except at home. When you get sufficiently confident about your craft, you might want to think about using it. My advice then is: forget you ever thought about using it.

Most literary novels choose the First Person these days, for good reason. Since character internality is the motor of literary plots, using First Person is a natural choice.

Third Person is most popular for thrillers and action driven books.

But this does not mean there is any one right answer. The right answer is what best fits your book.

Let's have a closer look at your alternatives:

1. First Person

First Person is the character telling us what happened.

I went to the store. I saw Frank. "What are you doing here?" I said.

Obviously, this POV requires everything to be seen through the eyes of one character. The Lead can only report what she saw, not what Frank saw or felt (unless Frank sees fit to report these items to the Lead). No scene can be described that the narrator has not witnessed—although you can have another character tell the narrator what happened in an "off screen scene."

You can use past or present tense with First Person POV. The traditional is past tense, where the narrator looks back and tells his story.

But the narrator can also do it this way: *I am going to the store. I see Frank. "What are you doing here?" I say.*

There is an immediacy of tone here that, when handled

well (as Steve Martini does in his Paul Mandarini legal thrillers) is quite compelling.

First Person makes for a very intimate, and potentially memorable, tale. But to do it well you have to create a strong, interesting voice for the narrator. Think *attitude*. The opening lines of *The Catcher in the Rye*, for instance, immediately tells us we're listening to someone with a unique view of his own life.

One can also choose to write First Person POV for various characters, in different chapters. Some authors put the name of the POV character at the start of the chapter, then proceed to write in that narrator's voice.

This requires skill, of course, because each voice must be different, each perspective unique.

2. Omniscient

The opposite of First Person, from an intimacy standpoint, is the Omniscient POV. Here you can go into any head, float around from a large scale description down to deep focus on any one character. This gives you great perspective, but at an intimacy cost. While introducing information is one of the benefits of omniscient, lack of focus is a possible drawback.

For example:

> Henry thought Rachel looked ravishing in her evening gown. He wanted nothing more than to wrap her in his arms and dance with her all night.
> Rachel saw that look in Henry's eyes and shuddered. How could she tell him that she had decided to marry Oswald?

Do you see how we have gone from one head to the other? (For further clarification on this, see the chapter on Head Hopping). *Technically speaking* "head hopping" is legit in Omniscient POV, but it seems from another age, the Victorian, where this kind of thing was done all the time. It's out of fashion now, readers preferring greater intimacy with a character.

There's a form of Omniscient POV we can call the *editorial*. This is where the author intrudes upon the narrative to make judgements or editorialize. It is clear to the reader that the author is speaking, rather than any character.

For example, Dickens' *David Copperfield* is told in First Person, from David's POV, so all the editorializing is via the character. But *A Tale of Two Cities* begins with these famous lines:

> It was the best of times, it was the worst of times, it was the age of wisdom, it was the age of foolishness, it was the epoch of belief, it was the epoch of incredulity, it was the season of Light, it was the season of Darkness, it was the spring of hope, it was the winter of despair, we had everything before us, we had nothing before us, we were all going direct to Heaven, we were all going direct the other way – in short, the period was so far like the present period, that some of its noisiest authorities insisted on its being received, for good or for evil, in the superlative degree of comparison only.

The editorial form is truly out of fashion now, but that doesn't mean a writer of a certain style of book couldn't use it. It calls attention to itself, so it is best utilized in a humorous or satirical novel (as in *The Hitchhiker's Guide to the Galaxy*).

A rare form of Omniscient POV is one where the action is described but no interior thoughts are rendered, nor descriptions of emotion. It's as if you were watching a movie, and a camera is set up to record the action. Because of its lack of intimacy, this was a popular form among the hard-boiled school of detective writers. Like Dashiell Hammett. Here's a clip from his classic, *The Maltese Falcon*:

> Spade sank into his swivel-chair, made a quarter turn to face her, smiled politely. He smiled without separating his lips. All the V's in his face grew longer.
> The tappity-tap-tap and the thin bell and muffled whir of Effie Perine's typewriting came through the closed door. Somewhere in a neighboring office a power-driven machine vibrated dully. On Spade's desk a limp cigarette smoldered in a brass tray filled with the remains of limp cigarettes.

Notice we are not in Spade's POV, because he would be unable to see the V's in his face grow longer. Nor do we get Spade's thoughts. And notice how the description of the cigarette on Spade's desk is like a camera zooming in. No wonder this book was so easy to film. It's almost like a shooting script.

Omniscient POV can be used selectively, such as in an epic tale, futuristic or historical. It's common for the author to build the world with Omniscience, and then "drop down" into the head of a character for the rest of the chapter or book.

3. Third Person

Third person comes in two varieties, limited and unlimited. Some call the latter "third person omniscient." To avoid confusion, I'm not going to do that. That's because with true omniscient you can "head hop" in a scene. With third person, you stay in one head throughout the scene.

If you use Third Person Limited, you are going to stay in one head for the entire book. Everything will be filtered through the main character. *Gone With the Wind* is this way. We experience everything (with a few minor exceptions) through Scarlett O'Hara.

With Third Person Unlimited, you can switch between characters from scene to scene or chapter to chapter. *The Stand* by Stephen King is like that.

13. Loose Ends

When a novel is finished readers want to feel one of two ways.

They want to go, *Ahh*.

Or, they want to go, *Uh-oh*.

What they absolutely do not want is to go, *Huh?*

The *Ahh* ending elicits a satisfied sigh that signals the book ended just right. It leaves a feeling of completeness. The best of these types of endings has the reader nodding and thinking there is nothing to add, no questions to ask, no loose ends to be tied up.

It's all here. I'm so glad I read this book!

Note, the *Ah* ending does not have to be a happy one. It's possible to end on a note of completeness but with a melancholy tinge to it. This can be true of classics like *The Hunchback of Notre Dame* or a "weepy" such as written by Mr. Nicholas Sparks.

The *Uh-oh* type of ending leaves the future a bit uncertain. The reason for that might be that the author wants to give you goosebumps, like Stephen King does so many times. Thus, at the end of the epic *The Stand,* there's a big *Uh-oh* that makes you think this whole thing could happen again!

Or, the author might be leaving it to the reader to fill in the future. That is the case with *The Catcher in the Rye*. Will Holden Caulfield ever make it out of that sanitarium? Will he ever be able to find meaning in life?

That's for us to ponder.

So, too, *Gone With the Wind*. Will Scarlett get Rhett back?

What makes the reader go *Huh?* is when there are loose ends that seem destined to dangle forever after the book is over. It means a question raised in the plot has not been answered, or if it has, the answer is a dud.

How do you avoid the *Huh?* type of ending?

Have your manuscript vetted by beta readers and a freelance editor. If some dangling threads are hanging there, tie them up by utilizing your minor characters.

One of those secondaries from somewhere in the middle of the book can come back into the proceedings to wrap up a loose end.

The character might:

- Provide information via dialogue.
- Cause everyone to think differently.
- Be the final piece in the puzzle.

What you do is come up with an ending that makes sense, using the minor character, then go back into your manuscript and put in the plot material that sets this up. In some cases you might not need any. In others, you'll need some foreshadowing or tweaking.

The nice thing is we can go back and forth in our novels whenever we want, for whatever reason.

Endings are the hardest part of the novel writing process. For me, at least. No matter how you've planned things, the novel takes organic shape as you write. New ideas pop up along the way. Characters make turns you didn't anticipate.

My approach to endings in general, and loose ends in particular, is to stew, brew, and do.

I think about the ending. A lot. Then I spend about an hour of heavy concentration on it.

Then I talk a walk, and let it all stew in the back of my mind. I listen to music. I enjoy the sun.

I end up at Starbucks and order an espresso. That's my brew.

Finally, I take out a little notebook from my back pocket and do: let the ideas flow from my subconscious. I'm not writing the actual ending. I'm just writing down what the boys in basement are tossing to me. I'll do mind maps, lists, even doodles.

Usually I wait a day before assessing any of it.

At last, I go to work on the ending, aiming for that perfect *Ah* or *Uh-oh*.

There's no better feeling in all of fiction writing than when you find that just-right ending.

14. No Push Through the Door

Structure is my beat.

My book, *Plot & Structure* (Writers' Digest Books) is the foundation. It was a labor of love from someone who was told you can't learn to be a writer, that the ability to plot was something you had to have born into you, that you might as well sling hash if you think you can write for a living without "it" being in you from birth.

I believed that twaddle for a long time. I lost ten good years of a writing life because of the chuckleheads who said you can't learn.

When I sat down to try—because I wanted to be a writer more than anything, and just had to give it a go, even if I failed—I began by studying structure.

At the time, the big structure book was *Screenplay* by Syd Field. Field said there were three acts in a good movie, with Act I comprising the first quarter of the running time, Act II half the time, and Act III the last quarter. He then determined there were two "plot points" that occurred to move the action from Act I to Act II, and from Act II to Act III. His "paradigm" looked like this:

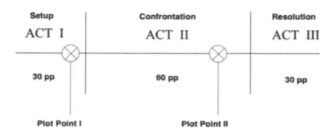

All well and good. But as I studied this out I got hung up on those plot points. What Field said they did was "spin the action around" into another direction. I could not figure out what that meant. Was it any random action? Because there are an infinite number of actions and an infinite number of directions a story can take.

Determined to find out what I was missing, I spent a year watching movies with a blank paradigm sheet in front of me. I divided the running time of a movie into quarters, and kept an eye on that first quarter, Act I, looking for the secret to the plot point.

I finally found it.

And dubbed it the "Doorway of No Return." The key is this: Something *pushes* the Lead into the confrontation with death (see Blunder #7). The Lead has to be forced through, because no one wants to fight with death. We want to stay in our nice, comfortable world and enjoy life as we know it.

We can't let that happen to the Lead! A novel or movie does not become *the story* until the Lead is forced to fight death, which is what Act II is all about.

Further, the Lead can't go back through the doorway to the old life. If she can, it's not a true break into Act II.

When you do this right, the reader will go right along with you.

But if you don't force entry into Act II, the story will feel weak. Unmotivated. Manipulative.

Note this, too. You must force that entry by the 1/5 mark of a novel or the 1/4 mark of a movie, or the book will start to drag.

Let's look at some examples:

The Wizard of Oz. At the 1/4 mark, Dorothy is taken, physically, to the Land of Oz. She can't go back through the Doorway. There is no return. She has to make it through the rest of the plot, and survive, in order to go back.

The Fugitive has the train wreck and escape in the first act. Then Tommy Lee Jones and his team of trackers show up. He immediately figures out Kimble has escaped. He orders roadblocks and a complete area search. "Your fugitive's name is Dr. Richard Kimble," he says. "Go get him."

That line is exactly one quarter of the way into the film. See what's happened? All the essential elements of the story are in place: escaped man and his opponent. They have competing agendas. Death is on the line. If Kimble is caught, he's toast. Death Row will be his final stop.

Gone With the Wind. After the first act, which sets up Scarlett and her ways and her obsession with Ashely, and her desire to live the life of the Old South and be a fine lady, something major forces her to fight for all that—the Civil War. She has no choice now. She has to fight. She can't go back to the old ways.

The first doorway can be an emotional push if it is strong enough to motivate the character into the death struggle.

That's what happens in *Star Wars.* Luke's Aunt Beru and Uncle Owen are murdered by Imperial stormtroopers searching for the droids C-3PO and R2-D2. Up to this point, Luke has only dreamed of going off on adventures. His loyalty to his aunt and uncle kept him on his home planet.

Now, though, he is experiencing loss and the desire to fight. He will go off with Obi-Wan Kenobi and learn the ways of the Jedi and join the rebellion.

The classic film *On the Waterfront* has an emotional push through the doorway. The movie is about a former boxer, Terry Malloy (Marlon Brando), who works now as an enforcer for the local crime boss. When the mob murders Joey Doyle, a friend of Terry's, because he's about to testify before a crime commission, Terry is troubled but still loyal to his "family."

Joey's sister, Edie (Eva Marie Saint), asks Terry for help in bringing the murderers to justice. At a local saloon Terry explains about life on the waterfront, how you have to stand with the right people so you have "a little change jinglin' in your pocket." And if you don't play by those rules you're going down.

Edie argues with Terry about his "living like an animal," but Terry insists that's better than ending up like her brother. He gets up to put on some jukebox music.

But he stops. He looks down at the distraught Edie.

Something happens inside him. It's a compassion he can't fight. It's the small shred of decency he has left in him. He's torn.

So instead of closing off this whole line of thinking, Terry follows his emotions and sits back down to comfort her.

This is the doorway of no return for Terry Malloy. He falls in love with Edie, and this forces an ultimate confrontation with the crime family. But it's mainly about his psychological struggle. Will he choose the "death" of being a thug forever? Or will he finally choose "life" by doing what is right and noble?

Ask yourself this: When does your Lead character get forced—by an action or strong emotion, or both—into the main conflict of your story?

Be clear in your own mind, and on the page so the reader will have no doubt.

Then place that scene before the 20% mark of your word count.

Do those two things, and your novel will not feel like a drag.

15. Chip on the Shoulder

Authors need a healthy ego, but not an inflated one.

If we think we don't need to learn anything, or are owed adulation simply because of the sparkling jewels we naturally are, then we have that proverbial chip on the shoulder, and that's not going to serve a writing career well.

There have been some famous egotist writers in the past. Hemingway wasn't exactly a shrinking violet. Norman Mailer didn't lack for self-esteem. Mailer was so pugnacious about being recognized as the great American author, he once wrote an article for a big magazine in which he has figuratively boxed with other writers like Hemingway and Steinbeck, and declared himself the winner.

The best thing for your writing, and your public image, is to be *confidently humble*. Write what you write, but be willing to make it better. Get your work to people who have a good eye—a critique partner, beta reader, or freelance editor. Fight for what you believe in, but only after you've given considerable time and attention to the suggestions that you get.

The chip-on-the-shoulder thing also applies to when you

get a negative review. You're a writer. You will get bad reviews. If you can't handle that, take up quilting instead.

Best strategy is not to read them. If you do read them, don't ever respond with vitriol. That will only make things worse.

Read your positive reviews on occasion, but don't dwell there. You should be writing instead.

Kipling called triumph and disaster two impostors, and said the key to life is to treat them just the same. Don't let either one of them rock your boat.

Keep an even keel, as the sailors used to say.

16. No Stinkin' Meaning

Theme.

It's something a lot of writers don't like to think about. It brings up painful memories of high school English class ("Write a 1,000 word essay on the theme of *The Great Gatsby,* and be sure to relate the green light on Daisy's dock with the eyes of Doctor T. J. Eckleburg. Due tomorrow.")

Which is why I prefer to speak of *meaning* instead.

You may be thinking, *I don't need no stinkin' meaning!* I just want to write with pedal to the metal and tell the story and let somebody else get a meaning if they want to.

And they will, whether you like it or not.

I think Chuck Palahniuk loves that people are fighting over the meaning of *Fight Club*. Maybe he had something in mind when he wrote it, and maybe he didn't. Perhaps the last person to trust on this is Chuck Palahniuk himself. Postmodern artists are puckish that way.

But what about you? Do you want the reader to feel something at the end of your novel? Do you want your story to be more than a sequence of events?

A great writing teacher of the mid-20th century, William

Foster-Harris, believed a story should be about two clashing values, with one of them coming out on top. So a story could be summarized this way:

Love v. Greed = Love

Which has a very different meaning than:

Love v. Greed = Greed

In the first case, love overcomes greed and the characters are happy at the end.

In the second, greed kills love, and the characters are unhappy at the end.

You should at least know what your story means to *you*. And then you can weave that meaning into your narrative.

Skillful weaving elevates a novel.

For example, the meaning of *To Kill a Mockingbird* is clear. It's even stated explicitly by Atticus. You don't really get to know a person until "you climb into his skin and walk around in it."

Did Harper Lee know this when she started the book? Perhaps. Or maybe it emerged more strongly as she worked on it, or after the first draft.

Regardless, throughout the book there are scenes that illuminate this meaning.

To the children, Jem and Scout, Mrs. Dubose is just a cranky old widow. But when she dies they find out she was fighting a morphine addiction with great courage. They think Dolphus Raymond is a hopeless drunk, only to discover he just drinks Coca-Cola.

Try this exercise. Go forward in time with your character at the end of the novel. If your character is dead, bring her back. Then ask the character: Why did you have to go through all that? What did you learn? What would you have us know about this lesson?

My friend Chris Vogler, author of *The Writer's Journey*, calls this the "return with the elixir." The hero has completed his journey, and the community receives the benefit of his wisdom, for the betterment of all.

Say Juliet, what did you learn? "Family hatreds will kill the ones you love."

And you, Sal Paradise, what did you learn out there on the road? "It's all about the beat, man, the experience. You gotta be one of the mad ones, the ones that go pop like a Roman Candle." (*On The Road* by Jack Kerouac)

Ms. Dagny Taggart, what about you? "Collectivism leeches off the ones who produce, and if they ever decide to say Forget that, we're not working for you anymore, you leeches won't know what to do as your world crumbles—as Atlas shrugs." (*Atlas Shrugged* by Ayn Rand)

George Bailey. Hey, George! I understand you now think it's a wonderful life. How'd that happen? "I learned you find your purpose in your own home town, by having friends and helping your neighbors. No man is a failure if he has friends." (*It's a Wonderful Life,* directed by Frank Capra)

Here's something you can do to give your story a nice, elegant arc.

Somewhere in Act I, have the character make an argument *against* the lesson they've learned by the end.

George Bailey does just that. It's in the scene where he, as a boy, is telling the two girls, Mary and Violet, that he's going to go see the world as soon as he can. He's going to become an explorer, and have a few wives, and maybe even a harem.

The movie becomes a transformative journey taking George from that position to the one he holds at the end.

In *The Wizard of Oz,* Dorothy learns "there's no place like home."

In Act I, she wishes she could go to a place far, far away, somewhere over the rainbow where there is no trouble. She wants it so much she even sings a song about it.

Try it. Readers will sense a deeper story going on.

Always a nice thing.

17. Letting Block Tackle You

So-called writer's block may be related to writer's fear (see the Fear chapter) or the writing blues (see the Quitting chapter).

But what happens when it feels like you just *can't* write?

Let's try to break it down into three broad categories: the new idea phase, the writing phase, and the excitement phase. In the first, your well seems to run dry. In the second, you seem to hit a wall. In the third, you just want to watch TCM with tortilla chips and a pitcher of margaritas.

Understanding which is which will help you get going again.

When Ideas Dry Up

This kind of block makes you feel like you have no good ideas left, no project that excites you.

Or maybe you have an idea, but you clutch at the prospect of writing it and wonder, if you do write it, if it will be worth it, if it will actually sell.

Maybe you feel like you have an "inner acquisitions editor"

who is looking at your idea and shaking her head, saying, "Sorry, I can't get this one past the pub board."

When this happens, you need to goose the muse. So—

1. *Write something really bad*

That's right. Bad. Really bad. Try to *make* it bad. You're going to find out something interesting: you have to *work* to write something really stinky. That's a confidence boost right there.

And it will be fun, too. You're going to like it:

> Dan Danger kicked in the door. The bad guys were all there, playing poker. Flat Head Muldoon reached inside his coat. Dan was faster. He pulled out his .38 and shot Flat Head through the heart. But Flat Head did not die. He was a zombie bad guy. He snarled at Dan and said, "I'm going to eat your brain."
>
> Dan said, "I have no brain," which was true, because Dan was really a Hollywood actor.

Or anything along those lines. It's just to get you writing again, feel the words come out of your fingers, and grease the wheels of your imagination.

Now write down ten things your imagination is telling you.

Then take one of those ideas and develop it into a story. Create an elevator pitch for it. Three paragraphs: 1) a character and situation; 2) the push into the plot; 3) the main story question. Like this:

> Dorothy Gale is a farm girl who dreams of getting out of Kansas to a land far, far away, where she and her dog will be safe from the likes of town busybody Miss Gulch.
>
> When a twister hits the farm, Dorothy is transported to a land of strange creatures and at least one wicked witch who wants to kill her.
>
> Now, with the help of three unlikely friends, Dorothy must find a way to destroy the wicked witch so the great wizard will send her back home.

You can do this for as many ideas as you like. You will soon be generating story-worthy ideas like a machine.

2. *The Dictionary Game*

I mentioned this in a previous chapter, as a way to get the unexpected into a scene. Use it now for ideas. Open a dictionary at random, find the first noun you see, and make up a story. Write at least one whole page (about 250 words), and see what happens.

Once you're past this type of block, you open yourself up to brainstorming again. Refer to the Brain chapter for more!

When You Hit the Wall

The other kind of block is the wall. That's when you're humming along on a project and all of a sudden you stop. You feel like you can't, or don't want to go on.

Early in my career I found I almost always hit this wall around the 30k word mark. I later found this to be true for other published writers. It's a curious phenomenon, perhaps because at that point we have passed the first "Doorway of No Return" and are bound to a story arc. Yet there is so much ahead, so many threads that will need to weave together. Add to that the pressure of wanting to make a good showing and you have a recipe for "freezing up," as golfers with the yips might say.

So I started doing what I called a 20k "step back," where I'd reach that point and do my own assessment of where the plot was going, make notes, outline some more, fix any major problems. Sort of a pre-emptive strike against "the wall."

When I started using Scrivener, I was able to generate an outline and synopses of scenes for what I *had* written. I could print that out, go sit in a comfortable chair, and read it over and think about it for a day, making new notes and so on.

One other trick is to imagine a writing mentor looking over my shoulder at this thing, and telling me what I might try. As in Raymond Chandler. He tamps his pipe, lights it, and says,

"Jim, you are not telling me enough about this guy. What's in his heart and his guts?" It's a way to get your right brain working again.

When You Lose the Excitement

You need to fall in love with writing again.

Try re-reading some favorite authors. This always gets me moving if I've got the writing blahs. I read some John D. Mac-Donald, Michael Connelly, Raymond Chandler, Stephen King, Tom Wolfe, Daphne DuMaurier, Edgar Rice Burroughs, Mickey Spillane.

It doesn't take long for me to want to get back to the keyboard.

A few other suggestions:

• Read an article in *Writer's Digest* (and subscribe to *Writer's Digest* so you have articles to read!)
• Every time you pick up a tip or technique, write it down in a notebook.
• Play an audio book as you exercise. Listen for the rhythm of the style as well as for the story.
• Go to a movie. If you love it, you'll want to write. If you hate it, you'll think *I can do better than that.*

18. Market Ignorance

There are two ways writers are functionally ignorant when it comes to markets.

The first way is to be obsessive about writing only what they think will sell big. I'm not saying that will never work. Indeed, certain genres—which shall remain nameless *cough* Monster Erotica *cough*—are little more than attempts—perfectly legal, mind you—to squeeze dollars from a segment of society that goes for such things.

If that's all you want to do, you're free to do it. But I call this a fiction writing blunder because almost always it doesn't make you a better writer. If you don't care to be a better writer, ignore this section.

The second form of market ignorance is … ignorance of markets. That is, writing with absolutely no thought about the readers on the other end. The writer doesn't give a rip.

That's fine, too. Some are happy to stay in that place. But it's a blunder if you want to write fiction as a vocation or career.

The sweet spot is somewhere in the middle. It's a spot that recognizes readers are consumers with preferences, but also that they look for, and respond to, an original voice.

It's the same calculation commercial publishers make when deciding what novels to take on. They want something fresh, but not so unique that it defies all market expectations.

Examples:

Stephen King in horror. He transcended and reestablished the genre because he was able to flow his enthusiasm and imagination into the work. He grew this market exponentially as a result.

Michael Connelly in detective fiction. You can tell that Harry Bosch is not some by-the-numbers cop. And he's grown more complex as this incredible series moves along.

John Grisham. He put more thrill into legal thrillers.

Janet Evanovich gave her bounty hunter, Stephanie Plum, a hilarious voice, and peopled the books with quirky characters. Readers have rewarded her by making her one of the bestselling authors of our time. Same for Nora Roberts and her J. D. Robb series.

Where is your sweet spot?

Find it. Nurture it.

Then take it to market.

19. Settling on First Ideas

When I say "Truck driver," what do you picture?

I'm sure most of you will see in your mind a burly fellow in blue jeans, a baseball or cowboy hat, maybe boots and a beard. Some variation on that theme.

That's because our minds are trained to give us the most familiar picture in our files, and we've all seen hundreds of truck drivers portrayed just like that.

In our writing—whether it be at the idea stage or in the heat of a scene—we are apt to follow that same pattern. We get an immediate picture based upon what we have experienced in the past. And usually it is quite in common with what so many other people have in their lives.

That's when you're in danger of writing a cliché. A cliché, after all, is merely something that is widely shared, repeated or experienced.

Your job as a creative writer is to stop yourself from repeating the familiar and find something original.

How do you do that?

Let me illustrate with a true story. It's about a man named Charles Townes. Never heard of him? He died in 2015 at the age of 99. He's the man who invented the laser, and is one of only two individuals to win both the Nobel Prize and the Templeton Prize. The other was Mother Teresa.

What's so interesting is how Townes came up with the idea. Here is a clip from the obit in the *Los Angeles Times*:

> [Townes] traced his seminal discovery of the maser to a "revelation" on a park bench in 1951.
>
> He had been working for years to decrease the wavelength of microwaves to enhance their use in communications and headed a Navy committee charged with solving the problem.
>
> Microwaves can have wavelengths as long as a few feet, but Townes was working with wavelengths of about half an inch and seeking still shorter ones, which would have more uses. But electronic devices that might generate such short wavelengths were too small to produce sufficient power for any foreseeable application.
>
> On the morning of the last day of a futile meeting in Washington, D.C., to consider new approaches to the problem, Townes sat on a park bench and contemplated the issue. He reasoned that developing electronic amplifiers would not work and started to imagine using molecules, which produce radiation when they vibrate at high speeds.
>
> The problem was that a lot of heat is normally required to make the molecules vibrate, and that heat destroys the molecules.
>
> He speculated that a flash of bright light could be used to create a population of excited ammonia molecules and that confining them in an appropriate cavity would limit the wavelengths that they could then emit.
>
> "So I took out a piece of paper and just scratched it out," he later said. Ultimately, he concluded, "Hey, this looks like it might work."

Don't you love that? One of the greatest scientific innovations of all time just came to Townes as he was sitting on a bench in a park. And then he starts "scratching" it out on paper.

Our subconscious mind is usually where our best ideas are housed, waiting to bubble up to the surface. We need to let them. And the way to do it is along the lines of what Townes experienced.

1. Concentration

The idea came to Townes after an intense morning meeting. But he'd also been thinking deeply about microwaves for years.

You first concentrate on your work-in-progress, whether it be big picture or small scene.

2. Relaxation

Next, get into relaxation mode. This can be as simple as some deep breathing. When I'm working on a major decision, such as an ending, I will often take a long, relaxing walk, letting my mind rest, until I end up at a Starbucks or a park bench to begin the next step.

If, on the other hand, I'm at a point in a scene where I need something unique or surprising, I'll take only a minute or two to relax and go to Step 3.

3. Recordation

Write down as many ideas as you can. There's a standard rule for creativity: the best way to get a good idea is to come up with lots of them, without judging, and later pick the best ones. Don't be afraid to write down even absurd, crazy notions. One of them may end up not being so crazy after all.

I like to use pen and paper for this. Sometimes I'll make a list of possibilities. Other times I'll generate a mind map on a single page. If you're not sure what a mind map is, take some time to learn and practice it. It's a fantastic way of getting creative. I first learned about it from Gabriele Rico's book, *Writing the Natural Way*.

4. Selection

The last step is to make your choice. Usually it's going to be one of the options you wrote after your initial thoughts.

It's quite interesting to note that Townes's colleagues at Columbia were skeptical of his idea. Niels Bohr, one of the great quantum physicists, and Nobel laureate Isadore Rabi, head of the university's physics department, told Townes his maser idea would never work and urged him to abandon the project.

He did not. And the rest is history.

You can follow this pattern in short bursts or longer periods. When you're coming up with a character, for example, don't grab the first picture that comes to your mind. Make a list of possibilities.

If your character is a truck driver, as I mentioned at the beginning of this chapter, reject that first image and start brainstorming. What else could he be?

- He could be skinny not burly, short not tall
- Maybe very short, needing a special booster to sit on
- A sensitive poet-type, doing this for money so he can write poetry at night
- He could be a *she*
- She could be a former ballet dancer now forced to drive a truck
- She could be the daughter of a legendary trucker
- She could be an undercover cop

That list took about one minute to generate and every one of the possibilities is better than that first cliché.

When you write a scene, you need to know the characters' agendas (see the chapter on Flabby Scenes). So why not spend a moment brainstorming other agendas? Invent a secret. Try the very opposite agenda and ask yourself if that can be justified.

20. Flabby Scenes

When southern California got hit with the big quake of '94, neighbors who had never spoken a word to each other suddenly could see into each others' backyards. That's because so many cinderblock walls crumbled to the ground. And the reason they did was that the walls, for the most part, were not built to withstand a quake of that magnitude. The blocks were not supported by rebar, nor were they of sufficient thickness.

Lesson learned. Countless walls, including my own, had to be rebuilt with sufficient support.

Scenes are the cinderblocks of your novel. They are the action that builds the tale and leads toward conclusion. But if they are not hearty enough to withstand the readers' demand to be entertained, the whole thing is liable to come down.

John Huston, the famous Hollywood film director, once counseled that a great film needs three strong scenes, and no weak ones.

Writers of fiction blunder when they allow weak scenes to remain. Such scenes need to be cut or revised.

What causes flabby scenes?

No tension or conflict.

Why wouldn't there be tension or conflict?

Puffing, for one. The writer feels he needs to expand the narrative a bit, or maybe "slow things down" for awhile.

But primarily there is a lack of focus on what the scene is really all about.

All Scenes Should Be About Conflicting Agendas

A scene is a unit of action within a larger narrative.

Every scene should have one viewpoint character through whom we "see" and experience the action. (Some writers will switch viewpoints within a scene, signaling that by way of a space break.)

Every character in every scene needs to want something.

Those wants need to be in conflict.

The viewpoint character should want something that helps further her cause in the story. She is in a death struggle, so is going to be acting, or reacting, in ways that help her overcome.

Let's say she's a lawyer. She has a client charged with murder and claims innocence via alibi. The client may or may not be lying. Professional death is on the line for the lawyer. If she can't win this case, she'll be let go from her law firm.

She wants to hire an investigator. So you write a scene where a male investigator comes to the lawyer's office for an interview.

What does she want? To find out if he's qualified.

What does he want? To lie to her.

Or maybe it's an investigator she's worked with before. But he has an alcohol problem.

Her agenda: determine if she can trust him.

His agenda: lie to her (he's really into lying).

She goes home to her lover. She wants to relax. It's been a rough day.

He wants to make love. Or wants to have a fight.

So pick opposing agendas. It is liposuction for flabby scenes.

Character Alone Scenes

Sometimes, of course, you'll have a scene with the character alone.

If the character is taking some action, put up obstacles to that action.

If the character is thinking, put up obstacles to that thinking—in the form of inner conflict.

A Great Source of Tension

My agent and teaching colleague, Donald Maass, preaches the value of "micro-tension." That means that every page—indeed, every beat on every page—contains some kind of conflict.

This conflict can be in the action, the dialogue, the inner thoughts, even the descriptive portions. It's a good goal to set for yourself, but how, exactly, do you accomplish it?

As I mentioned in the Marshmallow Dialogue chapter, one of the most useful tools for the writer is *fear*. It is the instant antidote to any flabby scene.

When someone is fearful, it means something is not right. The equilibrium of the world is disturbed. Happiness is on hold.

Which is always good for your scenes.

Go over your scenes in 100 word chunks. Make sure there is tension in every chunk.

If you can't find tension, cut the chunk or regroup and put some in.

21. Too Much in Love With Lyrical

In his introduction to Stephen King's first collection of short stories, *Night Shift,* John D. MacDonald explains what it takes to become a successful writer. Diligence, a love of words, and empathy for people are three big factors. But he sums up the primary element this way: "Story. Dammit, story!"

And what is story? It is, says MacDonald, "something happening to somebody you have been led to care about."

By *story* MacDonald did not mean some emotional mass springing fully formed, like Athena out of the forehead of Zeus. He meant plot, he meant craft, he meant effect, he meant connection with the reader.

Something happening is the soil in which plot is planted, watered, and harvested for glorious consumption by the reader. Without it, the reading experience can quickly become a dry biscuit, with no butter or honey in sight.

Mind you, there are readers who like dry biscuits. Just not many.

MacDonald reminds us that without the "something happening" you do not have story at all. What you have is a collection of words that may at times fly, but end up frustrating more than it entertains.

I thought of MacDonald's essay when I came across an amusing (at least to me) letter that had been written to James Joyce about his novel *Ulysses*. Amusing because the letter was penned by no less a luminary than Carl Jung, one of the giants of 20th century psychology.

Here, in part, is what Jung wrote to Joyce:

> I had an uncle whose thinking was always to the point. One day he stopped me on the street and asked, "Do you know how the devil tortures the souls in hell?" When I said no, he declared, "He keeps them waiting." And with that he walked away. This remark occurred to me when I was ploughing through Ulysses for the first time. Every sentence raises an expectation which is not fulfilled; finally, out of sheer resignation, you come to expect nothing any longer. Then, bit by bit, again to your horror, it dawns upon you that in all truth you have hit the nail on the head. It is actual fact that nothing happens and nothing comes of it, and yet a secret expectation at war with hopeless resignation drags the reader from page to page ... You read and read and read and you pretend to understand what you read. Occasionally you drop through an air pocket into another sentence, but when once the proper degree of resignation has been reached you accustom yourself to anything. So I, too, read to page one hundred and thirty-five with despair in my heart, falling asleep twice on the way ... Nothing comes to meet the reader, everything turns away from him, leaving him gaping after it. The book is always up and away, dissatisfied with itself, ironic, sardonic, virulent, contemptuous, sad, despairing, and bitter ...

Now, I'm no Joyce scholar, and I'm sure there are champions of *Ulysses* who might want to argue with Jung and maybe kick him in the id, but I think he speaks for the majority of those who made an attempt at reading the novel and felt that "nothing came to meet them."

I felt a bit of the same about the movie *Cake*, starring Jennifer Aniston. When the Oscar nominations came out that year it was said that Aniston was "snubbed" by not getting a nod. I entirely agree. Aniston is brilliant in this dramatic turn.

The problem the voters had, I think, is that the film feels more like a series of acting-school scenes than a coherently designed, three-act story. The effect is that after about thirty minutes the film begins to drag, even though Aniston is acting up a storm. Good acting is not enough to make a story.

Just as beautiful prose is not enough to make a novel. Years ago a certain writing instructor taught popular workshops on freeing up the mind and letting the words flow. It was good as far as it went, but this instructor taught nothing about plot or structure. Finally the day came when the instructor wrote a novel. It was highly anticipated, but ultimately tanked with critics and buyers. As I suspected, there were passages of great beauty and lyricism, but there was no compelling plot. No "something happening to someone we have been led to care about."

Of course, when beautiful prose meets a compelling character, and things do happen in a structured flow, you've got everything going for you. But prose should be the servant, not the master, of your tale.

Don't write to impress your readers. Write to distress your characters.

22. Competing the Wrong Way

I grew up competing in sports. Competition's always been part of me. It's a good thing, too. It leads to excellence in athletics, but also in life's pursuits.

That is, if you keep on the right side of it.

Because if you don't you can fall into a horrible trap—a "win at any cost" mentality. This is where you get rabid, idiotic parents at kids' baseball games who get into fights with other parents. Or coaches who will skirt the rules in order to gain a cheap victory. Or losers who refuse to shake the other player's hand.

It's also where you get writers who create sock puppet accounts so they can hammer their perceived rivals with bad reviews.

That's not true competition, which is based on a fair field. That's cheating, and if you allow yourself to do that you'll end up bitter, unpleasant to be around, and will probably have body odor, too.

So where does competition come in for the writer? We are in a solitary profession for the most part. We create our books in the quiet sanctuary of our office (or the more robust atmosphere of the coffee house). And then we prepare to release our work to the world—which may or may not be waiting for us with bated breath.

Does competition have any real meaning or purpose for the writer? I think it does, so long as you recognize the competition is really with yourself.

You're not involved in a zero-sum game where another writer must fail for you to succeed. You are in a race with only one person in it, you, and the object is to "better your time" each day.

To do that you have to create a standard of achievement. Then set goals based on that standard.

Let's say you are trying to land an agent. It's true you are in competition with other writers vying for the same thing. But the way you handle it is by looking at yourself objectively and figuring out how to become the sort of client an agent would want to handle.

It starts with your book.

Is the book the best you can make it? Did you have it assessed by a good freelance editor? Are you willing to take criticism and re-work your novel?

Have you put together a killer proposal? Do you even know what goes into a killer proposal?

Go into training and learn.

If you get rejected, regroup. Work on a new proposal, and submit again.

You do this until you win—get the agent—or decide to switch to a different field of play. Another agency, perhaps.

Or self-publishing. Then you establish a new standard and work toward that. Set goals for your quota, your study of the craft, your reading.

I do this annually. I look at my output over the last 12 months, then set my goals for the coming year. I look for areas to improve and make plans to improve them.

I don't worry about what other writers are doing. I'm not in competition with them.

Only with myself.

23. Clumsy Character Thoughts

Traditionally, there have been two ways to show a character thinking. You either do it with italicized lines, or unitalicized with the added attribution he thought or she thought. Thus, you might have the following:

> John walked into the room and saw Mary by the window. I wonder what she's doing here, he thought. [Note how the thought itself is in a first person voice]

> John walked into the room and saw Mary by the window. What was she doing here, he thought. [Note how the thought is now in a third person voice]

> John walked into the room and saw Mary by the window. *I wonder what she's doing here?*

You'll sometimes hear talk about "deep POV," which means we are so ensconced inside the viewpoint character's head that italics or attributions are not necessary. I'm not a stickler on this. I don't mind he thought or she thought on occasion, and don't think readers even notice. But it's worth, ahem, thinking about. If you've got a strong POV established, you can dispense with attributions and render the thought in a third- or first-person way:

> She opened the door. Saw his body. Bullet holes all over him.
> He deserved it, every bit of it.

> She opened the door. Saw his body. Bullet holes all over him.
> You deserve it, Frank, every bit of it.

On the matter of italics, it's become something of a meme among writers and writing groups that italics are out of date. I think that's mainly because italics can be abused. I've seen it done like this, and it always rubs me the wrong way:

> Rip looked at her with those cobalt blue eyes.
> Kiss me, kiss me now, oh please, I need to be kissed.
> "I like you, Dakota, I really do," Rip said.
> If you like me, go for it, my lips are ready for yours.
> "Do you like me too?" Rip asked.
> Like you! Can't you see it in my eyes? No, maybe he can't, because my heart has been broken so much it has grown calluses and become a hard, unnatural thing. Oh, break my heart, please break, so that you melt and warm my eyes for him, so he will take me in his arms and give me the love I have been yearning for.
> "Yes," Dakota said. "I like you."

Now, I don't mind a short, italicized thought when the emotions are running high. It's sometimes the best way to render the emotional impact on a character without stopping the flow of the action. Thus:

> He shoved her to the ground. Searing pain ran up her elbow and exploded at the base of her neck. She wanted to call for help, but her mouth wouldn't work. His laugh filled the void as he took off his mask.
> John!

Her former lover had...

Or:

"I hope you're happy," Max said.
    "Oh I am," said Constance. "So, so happy. Especially since you had the liposuction."
    He laughed then. And it chilled her to the bone.
    "Now," he said, "we are going to make love."
    Fat chance.

Sometimes, for stylistic reasons, you may want to try second person POV thoughts. Yes, that's what I said. It works if the emotion is running high.

He walked over to the window and looked at the street. A homeless guy was preaching to an invisible choir.
    Well, this isn't exactly what you wanted, is it? You wanted fame and fortune, and you got a cheap room in a crummy hotel, and you know you deserve it. Welcome to reality, pal. You done good, real good.

To sum up:

1. Use italicized thoughts sparingly, if at all. Save them for short, intense thoughts.

2. You don't need italics, or he thought/she thought if the POV is deeply established.

24. No Character Bonding

You need an opening disturbance. That will get your reader interested.

Then you need a character they bond with. That will get your reader invested.

Do those two things in your opening pages and you've got a true hook.

Why do readers bond with characters?

Because they want to worry. Readers plunk down their money for a book that will show a character in a death struggle. They will want to know how that struggle turns out.

If they are invested in the Lead.

With that in mind, what are some of the things you can do to create that crucial bond between reader and character?

Here are a few.

Imminent Danger

You can have a mother sitting in court, about to lose custody of her kids.

Or a father who has been told he's about to be fired, unless he shapes up.

Or a child who is kidnapped.

A cop who gets shot at.

A demolition man with a bomb.

A daughter with a domineering mother.

A cowboy with a domineering bull.

In short, you can place a character where something bad is happening, or about to happen. Readers will want to know what's going to happen.

Hardship

When a character is struggling with a hardship, readers respond with sympathy, because we all have issues ourselves.

Forrest Gump has both mental and physical hardships.

Frank Gavilin, the lawyer in *The Verdict*, struggles with drink.

Oliver Twist is a child in harsh circumstances from the get go.

One important note: the character in hardship shouldn't whine about it. He or she should not wallow in victimhood.

Underdog

We love the underdog story, the character who fights against long odds. Like Rudy, the small, academically-challenged kid who not only wanted to get into Notre Dame, but also play football there.

Or Rudy Baylor in John Grisham's *The Rainmaker*.

Or Katniss Everdeen in *The Hunger Games*.

Likability

We like rebels. Characters who stand up to illegitimate authority are likable because we desire to do the same thing!

We like characters with wit and self-deprecating humor.

We like guts.

We like rebelliousness.

We like people who care about someone other than themselves.

We like dreamers, as long as they don't live with their head in the clouds.

We like characters who will fight for what they believe in, unless what they believe in is evil, in which case we'll be wary and perhaps even scared of them (that's a good trait for your villains).

We like characters who don't give up.

Look at these qualities, like a checklist. It's okay to have a checklist of things that always work. That's what the craft of fiction is about.

Bond reader to character, keep it there for a whole book, then pay off that connection at the end.

That's the key to keeping readers happy, book after book.

25. Quitting

"Don't quit. It's very easy to quit during the first 10 years. Nobody cares whether you write or not, and it's very hard to write when nobody cares one way or the other. You can't get fired if you don't write, and most of the time you don't get rewarded if you do. But don't quit." —Andre Dubus

George Bernau was well-known lawyer in the San Diego area. He worked for a time in the same, big law firm where my brother is partner. In his thirties, working hard, climbing the ladder of success, Bernau got in a terrible traffic accident. In the emergency room he heard a doctor say he wasn't going to make it.

Death, as they say, was staring the lawyer right in the face.

But Bernau did pull through, and as he recuperated in the hospital he took stock of his life, did a total reassessment. He asked himself what he really wanted to do with his existence, and the answer was clear—write fiction.

With his wife's blessing, he transitioned out of the law and finished a novel. It stank. And he knew it stank.

Most first novels stink, by the way.

Bernau wondered what his next novel would be. He was talking to a friend one night about what life would have been like had President John F. Kennedy not been assassinated on November 22, 1963. An idea gripped him—write a novel with an alternate history, one where Kennedy survives.

He spent the next five years writing this novel, in longhand.

The novel, called *Promises to Keep,* was bought by Warner Books for a then-record advance for a debut author: $750,000.

Now what if that didn't happen? Let's do a little alternate history with George Bernau. What if his novel had been turned down all over New York?

Would he have quit writing?

Not a chance. In the hospital years earlier, Bernau said, "I decided that I would continue to write as long as I lived, even if I never sold one thing, because that was what I wanted out of my life."

There is no reason to quit writing. The worst that can happen to you is that you never make a single, solitary dime.

But here's the thing: if you refuse to quit, you will *certainly* make, at the very least, a single, solitary dime. There's real self-publishing income to be had, and even a ficus tree can make a dime.

You are more talented, more productive, and more resilient than a ficus tree.

Don't let a ficus tree show you up.

Never quit.

Beating the Blues

Every writer gets into the dumps from time to time. It's part and parcel of the creative life. The trick it not to let them beat you. I've found several things to be helpful in the doldrums.

1. Learn to be grateful for what you've got

So you've self-published a novel and have only five downloads this year. First of all, realize you have been given a gift, the gift of getting your book out there for potential readers, of which you now have five (and yes, we WILL count your brother-in-law). Start by being grateful that you can type, that you can tell stories, that your imagination is on the move. And that you can learn to be a better writer. Which leads to:

2. Set up and follow a rigorous self-study program

When you work at something, you're being proactive. Activity is one sure way to drive the blues away.

So study your craft. I just do not get the people who say you can't learn how to write by study and practice.

Do we say that to doctors? Or plumbers?

All the writers I know who have made something of themselves have been students of their craft. They read books and go to conferences and are in critique groups and hire editors. They spend part of every day thinking about what they do and how they can do it better.

Take an objective look at your writing (you may need an outside source, like a freelance editor, for this). Determine the three weakest areas in your writing (Plotting? Style? Characterization? Dialogue?) and then find resources on them and study them out. Practice the techniques you learn.

I guarantee it will make you feel better. I love the craft and still diligently study it, but also remember this:

3. Write wild on your first drafts

Despite persistent internet claims to the contrary, Hemingway never said that writing means you sit down at the typewriter and bleed (it was actually sports writer Red Smith who talked about "opening a vein"). But it's a proper sentiment for the writer. Give each scene you write the most creative and wild investment that you can. Get into "flow" by "being here now." When you are in the zone, the blues disappear.

You all know about that "inner editor" that needs to be silenced when you write. Don't think too much when you're actually composing. That was Ray Bradbury's great advice. He would start writing in the morning and "explode." Then he spent the latter part of the day picking up the pieces.

Write hot. Then edit cool.

4. *Know you are not alone*

If you haven't already, sometime soon you'll get a case of the "review blues." You are in good company. Even some of the best books of all time have their critics.

All writers (with the possible exception of Lee Child and Stephen King) face the-lack-of-sales blues, the envy-blues, the who-am-I-fooling blues and variations thereon. Which is why many a writer of the past turned to the demon rum for solace. Bad bargain. Instead:

5. *Try exercise*

It works. Get those endorphins pumping.

Another thing I do between writing stints: lie on the floor with my feet up on a chair. Then deep breathe and relax for about ten minutes. The blood flows to the gray cells and gives them a bath. The boys in the basement get to work. And I feel energized when I get up.

You're a storyteller and the world needs stories—even if you have to slog through the swamp of melancholy to tell them. In fact, it may be that this very dolefulness is the mark of the true artist.

So stay true. Stay focused. And keep writing.

26. No Strength of Will

One way I define a novel is that it is *the record of how a charac-ter, through strength of will, fights with death.*

We've already covered death stakes.

Now it's time to deal with how a character responds.

When I teach how to come up with a great Lead character, my first rule is: No wimps!

What is a wimp? Someone who sits there and takes it.

Someone who is reacting, not acting.

It's all right for a character to start out as a wimp. But very quickly you must show that he has a capacity for change, and will be challenged to change soon.

Stephen King's *Rose Madder* is a novel about a horribly abused wife. Her husband is a psycho cop who beats her and keeps her a virtual prisoner. King gives us a graphic prologue to show us all this.

But if King were to continue with more of the same, we would quickly be turned off. Instead, he ends the prologue with these chilling words: *Rose McLendon Daniels slept within her hus-band's madness for nine more years.*

We turn the page and King gives us a little bit of narrative summary of those years. But then he tells us that Rose "awakened" finally from this nightmare: *What woke her up was a single drop of blood, no larger than a dime.*

> She looked at the spot of blood, feeling unaccustomed resentment throbbing in her head, feeling something else, a pins-and-needles tingle, not knowing this was the way you felt when you finally woke up.

And this is what finally prompts her to action—to leaving the house for the first time, despite her husband's warnings that he would kill her if she did.

This is Rose showing strength of will. And that's what gets the motor running.

Don't ever let your Lead stay in a reactive mode for very long.

Even as you move through Act II, the heart of the story, don't let the rest stops linger.

In the movie *Rocky* (the first one, the best one), the showboating heavyweight champ Apollo Creed is clowning around in the ring as he fights the guy he thought was just a bum, Rocky Balboa. Only Rocky has taken this fight seriously, gone into strict training, and he's starting to hurt Creed.

At one point Creed's corner man looks at the champ's puffy face and screams, "He doesn't know it's a damn show! He thinks it's a damn fight!"

That's what your novel is. It's not a show. It's a fight.

Get your characters into a fighting spirit, and soon.

27. Bland Minor Characters

Don't waste your minor characters!
Don't give them a few stereotypical lines and then toss them into the story. And out again.

Minor characters are a fantastic way to pump up your novel and add more reading pleasure for the reader.

Which is what you want, right?

I see a lot of bland minor characters in manuscripts. The usual reason is that the author has grabbed the first image he sees and put it on the page.

For instance, when I say think of a *bartender*, what do you see? My guess is the first image is of a man. Depending on the kind of bar you frequent, it could be a beefy man wiping a glass, or one of those Tom Cruise types throwing bottles around.

The point is, you've seen it before, and so have readers.

What if I say *librarian?* I'm almost positive you saw a woman. Probably wearing glasses. And if you're old school enough, maybe with a pencil stuck in the bun in her hair!

Seen it!

So the first thing to do with a minor character is *reject the obvious*. It will take you about thirty seconds to do that and come up with something a little more original.

Try flipping it. Think of the very opposite.

Try making the character the opposite sex.

The opposite look and build.

Another skin color.

Or hair color.

Or fingernail color.

Play around and see what your mind comes up with.

You can start extreme. Go to the max. Make the character as wild and crazy as possible—then pull back until you get the right tone.

In Michael Avallone's detective novel, *The Case of the Bouncing Betty* (1956), PI Ed Noon comes across a 440 pound woman who works as a "mattress tester."

You just don't forget these things.

Minor characters can be the spice that makes the meal not just satisfying, but memorable. Minor characters should be the cilantro of fiction, the nutmeg of narrative.

There's a reason we read more Dickens than we do Trollope.

It's because of the minor characters.

BONUS:
Getting Started With Scrivener

I want to say a few words about Scrivener. No doubt you've already heard about it from a writing friend, or by reading about it online.

You may even have tried it out but gave up when you saw how many features it has.

Yes, Scrivener does have a lot of "bells and whistles" that can, if taken in all at once, make someone think, "Sheesh! I can't possibly learn this!"

So ... don't take in everything at once! Scrivener is actually simple to use for many cool functions. Any other stuff can be learned at your leisure. (See the end of this post for my recommendation on that).

Here is how I advise approaching Scrivener when you first get it:

1. Think of it as a binder

Many writers of the past used physical notebooks to house their drafts, notes, research and other items. I'm sure some still do. Well, Scrivener is a digital binder. Everything you generate can be stored here.

My binder always has my scene cards, the manuscript itself, character cards (with head shots), research, clippings (a cool feature is that you can highlight something on the internet and send that to a clippings file in Scrivener), and my novel journal.

All of this material is, of course, searchable.

2. Think of it as a creativity booster

One of my favorite features in Scrivener is the corkboard. It's just like the one in your office, with the push pins, only this one is virtual. I usually start my projects by thinking up random scenes, jotting notes on Scrivener's "index cards" and "pinning" them on the corkboard. I can then move them around as I like. Below is a screen shot of a made-up project I created for a presentation:

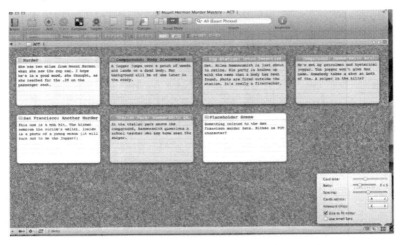

The jottings you see on the index cards are the synopses. Later, if you wish, you can compile only these jottings and voila! You have a synopsis of the whole project.

You can see that the cards are different colors. You can

select what colors you want them to be. I choose colors by subplot.

You can create your own templates in Scrivener. I have one for my character work. It contains the key questions I ask about each main character.

One tool I use all the time is Scrivener's name generator. Set your parameters (e.g., nationalities, male or female, etc.) and the name generator will give you hundreds of suggestions with just one click.

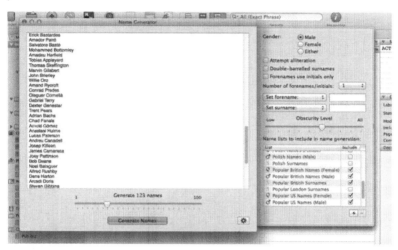

3. Think of it as an organizer

Scrivener lets you organize your project, and view it, in many ways.

I like to use folders for Act 1, Act 2, and Act 3. When I create a scene card, I can put it into the folder where I think it will logically fit. I can organize the scenes within the folders all I want, moving them around on the corkboard, or up and down on the left side panel.

There's an outline view that's extremely helpful in letting you know where you are in your WIP. The corkboard view I shared, above, looks like this in outline view:

The same color codes are there, and the same synopses. When you have a lot of scenes, you can look at the colors and decide if you need a yellow scene here, or a blue scene there.

If you are a "plotter," you'll naturally love all this. But "pantsers" will too! Why? Because you pantsers get all sorts of wild ideas as you write. So what do you do about them? You can jot scene ideas on an index card, even write some of that scene, and put it into a folder for later reference. You can move those cards around as you please. Then, when it comes time to bring a little order to your mess, Scrivener will help you do it.

4. Think of it as a word processor

You could use Scrivener for all of the above, and still choose to write your manuscript in Word. Even then, Scrivener is worth the price for the reasons mentioned above.

But you can also draft your books right in Scrivener. When you're done, you can export your book as a Word document, ebook ready .mobi and .epub formats, and print-ready pdf (e.g., for CreateSpace).

Okay, I've tried in this short space to give you an idea of what you can do with Scrivener right from the jump. So, once again, don't let all the features intimidate you. You can learn as you go.

There are tutorial videos available for free at the sales site. And books, such as *Scrivener for Dummies*. Bottom line, even if you get Scrivener and use it only to help plan, organize, and store your research, it's a good investment. But if you decide to use it to write and create your own e- and print books, you'll soon appreciate its power.

Helpful Stuff for Writers

I've been at this game for a long time now, professionally published and teaching writers, through books and workshops, all over the world. There aren't many writing or publishing challenges I haven't faced and figured out how to meet.

That's why I write about the craft. I love helping writers, because I know where you've been.

So below I've listed my books by subject matter for your continuing success.

First, though, please take a moment to sign up for my email updates. You'll be the first to know about my book releases and special deals. My emails are short and I won't stuff your mailbox, and you can certainly unsubscribe at any time. If you do sign up, I'll put your name in the random drawing I do each month for a free book of mine.

Sign up by going to my website: www.jamesscottbell.com. And keep writing!

Plot & Structure

Write Your Novel From the Middle
Plot & Structure
Super Structure
Conflict & Suspense

Revision

Revision & Self-Editing

Dialogue

How to Write Dazzling Dialogue

Publishing & Career

How to Make a Living as a Writer
The Art of War for Writers
Self-Publishing Attack!

Writing & The Writing Life

Writing Fiction for All You're Worth
Fiction Attack!

My Blog

Killzoneblog.com

Made in the USA
San Bernardino, CA
24 July 2015